Facing
Double-Edged
Sword

ONE ENCOUNTER
ONE CHANCE

Facing the Double-Edged Sword

THE ESSENCE OF TAKE NAMI DO KARATE

TERRENCE WEBSTER-DOYLE

ONE ENCOUNTER ONE CHANCE
Facing the Double-Edged Sword
The Essence of Take Nami Do Karate

by Terrence Webster-Doyle

Co-Publisher's Addresses:

The Shuhari Institute/Atrium Society
P.O. Box 938
Ojai, CA 93023

North Atlantic Books
2320 Blake Street
Berkeley, CA 94704

Art Direction: The Illusionist
Production Coordination: Shari Mueller
Laser Typography: John Shoolery
Creative Consultant: Jean Webster-Doyle
Cover Concept: Shari Mueller
Cover Photography: Kim Stephenson
Inside Photography: Earl Bates, Timothy Teague,
Cheryl A. Traendly

Special Thanks to Take Nami Do Instructors:
Jeff Greene, Steph Snedden, Stan James

Library of Congress Cataloging in Publication Data
Webster-Doyle, Terrence, 1940-
    One Encounter — One Chance.

    1. Karate — Philosophy. 2. Self-knowledge, Theory of.
    Self-defense — Psychological aspects. I. Title.

GV1114.3.W43   1987   796.8'153   87-23246

ISBN 1-556430-14-0
ISBN 1-556430-13-2 (pbk.)

Table of Contents

"The present just as it is is the reality of our ideal world."

— Anonymous

Facing the Double-Edged Sword

A soldier named Nobushige came to Hakuin, and asked: "Is there really a paradise and a hell?"

"Who are you?" inquired Hakuin.

"I am a Samurai," the warrior replied.

"You are a soldier!" exclaimed Hakuin. "What kind of ruler would have you as his guard? Your face looks like that of a beggar."

Nobushige became so angry that he began to draw his sword, but Hakuin continued: "So you have a sword! Your weapon is probably too dull to cut off my head."

As Nobushige drew his sword Hakuin remarked: "Here open the gates of Hell!"

At these words the Samurai, perceiving the teacher's discipline, sheathed his sword and bowed.

"Here open the gates to paradise," said Hakuin.

— Zen Flesh-Zen Bones by Paul Reps

This book is the foundation book for Take Nami Do Karate. It is not a manual on self-defense techniques. Rather, more importantly, it is an inquiry into this unique style's emphasis on self-understanding through the intelligent practice of the Art of Karate. This book takes a new look at the traditional principles of Karate and gives the reader an insight into their original meaning as they are portrayed in this particular form.

The essence of Take Nami Do Karate is "Facing the Double-Edged Sword." The sword is a metaphor for the mind that can cut through the knots of its own confusion, the conditioned attitudes mankind has about living—or—conversely, being slain by the destructive nature of habitual, conditioned thinking.

People usually live half-heartedly, not really giving of

themselves. "Living under the sword," one is forced to live fully, to give totally. Time is the slayer of the mind, for it is postponement; it is the effort of the will to overcome its own self-made prison.

There is only the present moment, the now. There is only One Encounter, One Chance for the mind to act without hesitation, alert to the danger of the cutting edge, the danger of the many precarious challenges of life. The practice of the Art of Karate develops acute perception, a heightened sense of alertness that can penetrate the illusions created by confused thinking, illusions that are the outcome of destructive behavior.

Through the training cultivated by learning the skills of defending oneself from physical assault, the mind/body becomes alert, razor-sharp, capable of dealing intelligently with the threat of being attacked. This skill goes beyond the physical threat into the psychological realm, where a highly perceptive mind is needed to discern the psychic attack, the attack of the confused and dangerous individual lost in the destructive patterns of convoluted thinking. The keen and razor-sharp mind sees the attack, sees the opponent's confused state and can therefore act intelligently to disarm the potential threat. Being free of the attack the student of Karate can respond with fearlessness, whereas before he or she might have reacted out of fear, and counter-attacked, creating a vicious circle of aggression. Not being caught up in the attack the student is free to deal more constructively with hostility. This is the essence of creative self-defense. The student wins by losing, by not becoming a victim of provocation. In this space created between the action of attack and the reaction out of fear, there is intelligence. It is this space of intelligence that every student of Karate must understand in order to master the Art. It is the heart of the practice.

One Encounter, One Chance lays the foundation for the study of Take Nami Do Karate as a means of understanding the self, understanding the violent world in which we live. It is a book that begins to explore the roots of conflict that goes beyond the traditional forms of Karate and asks the reader to let go of preconceived notions so he or she can see the real intention of this remarkable Martial Art.

INTRODUCTION

"The action we think will free us is the very action that is
destroying us. Trying to become nonviolent is itself violence
because it is based on the ideal."

— Terrence Webster-Doyle

Many people are looking for a way, a method, to solve
their problems. Many people have become disillusioned with
conventional religion as an answer to their problems. Some
people have turned to the Martial Arts, Karate in this case, as
a new way to solve their problems. If they are drawn to the
Martial Arts for the same reason they were formerly drawn to
religion, there is a very dangerous and tragic irony here. We
could be promoting much more violence in the world by
practicing the Martial Arts as a form of religious practice.

What is dangerous is *how* we approach solving our problems. The "how" implies a method, a way to do something
about them, which means creating the ideal, a should, and
the effort to attain that. This dilemma which seems so simple
is of utmost importance. I am not being philosophical or
intellectual. I am interested in reality, in actually understanding how we can change behavior and the violence in relationship. The traditional approach to solving our psychological
problems has paradoxically created more violence. In other
words, our very approach to solving these problems is violent,
because it is based on the ideal, on trying to be what we are
not through suppression and conformity.

As an Instructor in the Art of Karate I am aware that the
Martial Arts have the potential to perpetuate the same cycle.
Japanese Karate, for example is founded in Zen Buddhism; it
promises enlightenment, a way to be free of the self, the "me"
with all my problems. This attitude has been carried over into
the functional practice of Karate today, subtly or overtly. The
attainment of enlightenment is based on control, on being
disciplined. Discipline here has been translated into setting a
goal and putting aside all other distractions. In the case of

enlightenment the goal is the annihilation of the self, which is the source of psychological conflict. The process of ending the self is to practice, practice, practice and control, control, control. In Zen it is to sit, sit sit. This rote practice is thought to be a way to control the emotion (which is a part of the self) including any display of genuine feeling. It often results in a literally emotionless, hard person incapable of real feelings like love, sadness or joy. Emotions, the "feelings" manifestation of the self, are viewed somewhat like a wild horse that needs to be broken. The thinker, the me, the one who wants to be enlightened, is the rodeo rider who will climb on the back of the wild steed (the self) and hold on for dear life no matter what happens (which is the discipline). But the paradox is that the rider and the wild stallion are one and the same! In other words, the self is riding the self, or itself, thinking that there are actually different selves: the rider (the thinker, controller) and the self (the wild thoughts and emotions that need disciplining, taming).

I find that traditional Karate is very much like traditional religion: they both are belief systems based on following the letter of the law; they both employ what we call a "fundamentalist approach." The basic structure is simple: just do it exactly one way—never deviate and never question! There is a logic to this fundamentalism, one that appeals to people who are frightened. It is that there will be someone who will take care of them if they just do exactly as they are told. This is obviously a very childish approach. All they have to do is obey. It creates more conformity, more dependence and therefore more conflict. Conflict comes about when we deny our own intelligence through strict conformity to another.

This does not mean that one must rebel against authority. There is a place for the tradition and knowledge of the authority. We can learn from teachers. What really has to happen is that we need to learn from tradition and at some point bring our own intelligence, or insight, into our practice. This intelligence, which is awareness or the ability to focus attention, is what will bring about a balanced and healthy practice.

In Take Nami Do Karate we recognize the inherent problem in rigid conformity to ideals, in trying to discipline ourselves for the ideal of enlightenment, thereby creating the division in oneself as the controller and the wild horse that needs to be controlled. We practice with this paradox consciously in mind. The most essential element in Take Nami Do is focus (Kime). Focus is simply bringing attention to whatever is at hand. This sounds easy but it is the most difficult thing to do because we are fragmented. Fragmented means that we are divided and hence in conflict. Our division is caused by using a method, by the process of trying to change behavior, through ideals. Because we are divided and in conflict our energy is dissipated, fragmented, used up in the effort it takes to maintain the struggle to become, to eliminate the negative and accumulate the positive. Being fragmented we cannot focus. Focus means *undivided* attention.

In Take Nami Do we bring these issues to our attention because we see the vital importance in understanding them; we see that understanding these issues is what the Art of Karate is really about, as perhaps the original intention of religion was about before it became lost in ideals, in the seeming security of dogmatic assertion of beliefs. We are concerned with this basic fragmentation and the conflict it creates because it is the root of psychological disorder. We see that without understanding this fundamental problem we will just be creating more violence, especially in learning Karate. Karate is very powerful because it touches on the deepest fears and primal instincts. We are aware of how careful we need to be, especially in teaching young people. Understanding all this, our intention must be to create a context, an environment where we can explore ourselves, explore this tendency to try to solve our problems through ideals. This context or environment will allow us to look at who we are without the ideal, to observe ourselves as we actually are, without judgment.

The traditional approach to ending our problems is through the creation of ideals, as we have said. This means judgment, labeling what we see (the quality we want to change) as bad and then creating our idealized image of goodness to conform to. This division, and hence struggle, between the good and bad creates the structural basis of this conflicting process. In the context Take Nami Do Karate creates we have the opportunity actually to be what we are. When we focus just on this, when we are aware of who we are without the conflict of judgment, then there is understanding. Understanding is being able to look at the fact, to come into direct contact with what it is. This observation without judgment is understanding.

At first we start focusing on simple things, like sitting or practicing basic self-defense movements. It is easier to start with the physical, with the body, and then to move from there to the more complex. We have built up a strong defense system, because of the pain of being hurt, the pain of judging ourselves, so it is sometimes hard at first to look at who we are. The transformation usually comes about slowly, although it is not actually a process of time. Who we are is always available to see at any time and it is only seeing in the moment that will bring understanding and the ending of conflict. Slowly means that we are not immediately ready to drop our defenses; we first need some confidence. This confidence comes from the nonjudgmental and controlled environment Take Nami Do Karate creates. "Controlled" here means that the limitations of what we are allowed to do in Karate are clear and straightforward for all to see. When a person understands his or her limits, understands just how far he or she can go in expressing him- or herself, then he or she is free to explore in the safety of that limitation. Pulling punches or kicks just short of the intended target, the student is allowed to experience the intensity of a full power technique and at the same time experience the control of the limit set upon the technique. This allows the student to go full out but also allows him or her the safety of knowing where and when to stop. This ability takes great focus, being able to concentrate on the Karate form. This focus is on the physical aspects of Karate. But focus is much more than this.

What if the student is not focused? What brings about focus in the student if he or she is fragmented and divided? Can we create a fire, create a challenge in training so vital that it brings the student's attention to the urgency of needing to understand the problem?

In the allegorical Martial Arts stories the teacher, seeing the need to create this fire, makes the problem greater, exacerbates or irritates the problem to such a degree that the student is at such a pitch of frenzy he or she must have the intensity and seriousness to end it.

In Take Nami Do Karate, as in life, we must create this state of emergency, this fire, to bring the challenge of self-understanding to such a state of urgency that we drop all our resistances, our escapes and defenses, and come to face the problem immediately. The problem of relationship is itself a state of emergency! We don't have endless time to solve it. Take Nami Do Karate is a vehicle, a context, in which we can come into direct contact with who we are.

Take Nami Do is not a new style, a new way. It only allows one to bring focus, attention without judgment, to what is. It is the focused attention that will paradoxically act as a flame to burn through the resistance and bring an end to the psychological and hence social disorder.

Take Nami Do Karate brings the student's awareness to the challenge of the double-edged sword. In Take Nami Do we use the double-edged sword as a metaphor for focus, for attention on the one side of the blade and ignorance or inattention on the other. One side of the sword can free by cutting through the knot of confusion, while the other side can cut and "kill" through the lack of attention.

In Karate one trains in the Art of Self-Defense. Through the training developed in learning the skills of defending oneself from physical assault, the mind/body becomes highly alert, capable of dealing appropriately with the threat of being attacked. If one is thinking of winning or losing then one is lost and will be "cut" by the enemy. If one is attentive and alert then one's response will only be from the razor-sharp clarity of the moment, from blending with the opponent's attack and in so doing, rendering him or her harmless. Here we use the sword of awareness to cut through the fear generated in the opponent as well and in so doing, bring him or her back to his or her senses, into the freedom of the moment. In this there is no time, no movement of thought for self-survival. There is only the immediacy of the moment, there is only **One Encounter** and only **One Chance** to respond either intelligently through understanding or unintelligently through fear. When there is an attack one has only a single moment to respond appropriately to disarm the opponent.

Rendering an opponent harmless does not mean one uses force, counter-attacking by raw physical means. On the cutting edge of awareness, one can use an endless array of means to avoid or neutralize an attack. When we are alert, alertness itself is energy. This energy can be enough of a deterrent to divert potential aggression. Alertness can also aid us in employing a variety of nonviolent alternatives to transform hostile aggression. Not letting the cutting force of fear immobilize oneself, one has the opportunity to respond intelligently in the momentary space created between the hostile action and the defensive reaction.

Beyond the potential for physical assault (which, after all is not generally a frequent occurrence in one's daily life), the cutting edge is mirrored in the psychological realm where a highly perceptive mind is needed to discern the psychic attack, the attack of the confused and dangerous mind that is lost in the destructive patterns of knotlike, convoluted or idealistic thinking. The keen and razor-sharp mind of the sword sees clearly the fear and the potential for attack, the opponent's confused state, and can therefore act intelligently to disarm the possible threat. Being free of the attack one can respond with fearlessness, whereas before he or she might have reacted out of fear and counter-attacked, contributing to a vicious circle of violence. The student, not being caught up in the attack, not being "cut" and hurt psychologically and therefore wanting to cut and hurt back, is free to deal more constructively with hostility. This is the essence of creative self-defense. The student "wins by losing," by not becoming a victim of provocation. In this space created between the action of attack and the reaction out of fear, there is intelligence. It is this space of intelligence that every student of Take Nami Do Karate must understand in order to master the Art. It is the heart of the practice.

The psychological attack, so to speak, comes from within oneself as well as from another. It comes in reaction to the attack from outside as well as from its own self-generated fears. The fundamental fear is the fear of self-survival, the fear of losing control, of being nothing. This root fear generates a host of related fears that seem to plague the mind constantly—"Will I lose my job, my wife, my money, my home? Will I get sick or hurt?"—all the many fears related to one's self, which ultimately is the fear of death...not physical death, but the death of the self, the psychological accumulation called "me," "I." One side of the double-edged sword cuts into the integrity and sanctity of the moment, bringing fear and immobilizing the person. We live in fear, in the thoughts of self-preservation, in the anxiety that at any moment we may lose everything. The attentive and intelligent mind, seeing that the sword's edge is not real, that it is *only* thoughts, is not cut because the awareness has blunted the cutting edge. Awareness has seen through the attack and in so doing, it has dissipated the possibility of the danger. This alertness is the other side of the sword, the mind's ability to discern between a real threat and the bogus enemy.

The traditional warrior-like approach to resolving conflict is through counter-aggression, an eye for an eye approach. When one attacks, the other counters by defending and violently counter-attacking. This is seen not only on the personal, individual level but also on the global level. The serious student in the Art of Karate develops confidence from the tradition of learning self-defense skills but goes further in his or her understanding of the nature and structure of violence. In understanding aggression, the student of the Art of Karate doesn't employ the old strategies of violent counter-aggression because he or she understands that they have never worked, that they only perpetuate violence. The student of the Art of Karate prepares him- or herself for the real battle, for winning by losing, for he or she knows that this is the most intelligent strategy for success. The student of the Art of Karate, because he or she is confident, can respond creatively to potential conflict, whereas the traditional approach is "might is right" and brute force to intimidate. The student of the Art of Karate's weapon is the cutting edge of the sword of awareness. The student of the Art of Karate is a Warrior of peace because he or she has faced the problem and understands it, and in so doing, does not perpetuate it within him- or herself or within the world.

In the Art of Karate, what others see as combat is only the pure expression of energy in form. It is not violence, yet it may seem so to those who take refuge in the conflict of nonviolent ideals.

PART I
THE WAR WITHIN
UNDERSTANDING THE ROOTS OF CONFLICT

"Projection makes perception. The world you see is what you make of it. Nothing more than that...It is the witness of your state of mind, the outside picture of an inward condition. As a man thinketh, so does he perceive. Therefore, seek not to change the world, but choose to change your mind about the world."
—**Anonymous**

It is necessary to have a fundamental understanding of Karate and the Martial Arts if one's practice is going to be intelligent. Without a basic insight into the nature and structure of conflict, the student of the Martial Arts will only add more violence to the world.

Most Martial Arts books offer only self-defense techniques as a type of physical panacea for the problem of violence. If they offer any insight into their Art it is usually a superficial historical or cultural view of a particular form. Rarely do books on Martial Arts explore the roots of conflict.

One Encounter— One Chance: Facing the Double-Edged Sword, The Essence of Take Nami Do Karate is a book intended to inquire into the real basics of Karate as an Art of Empty Self.

The intention of Take Nami Do Karate is to educate the students to a fundamental understanding of conflict, for without an insight into its causes, one can only perpetuate it, thereby compounding the problem. What is presented in the following pages is a collection of observations on the nature and structure of the roots of conflict. These observations are offered as a working hypothesis only, as a stimulation for inquiry. The observations are not conclusions, dogmatic assertions by the author, or dictates a student should follow. They are only a means by which others can begin to look for themselves.

Too often books are written as bibles, as authoritative texts to memorize and to emulate. The intention of this book, using the medium of Take Nami Do Karate, is to create a mirror of oneself in relationship. Take Nami Do Karate allows the student, because of the safe and trusting environment it fosters, to explore him- or herself. The practice of self-defense skills can bring up to the surface once hidden or repressed emotions. Allowing these emotions to surface into the light of awareness, without the interference of judgment, is the curative process of the Art of Take Nami Do Karate. These repressed feelings have been controlling behavior in an undercurrent of self-destructive ways. Creating a context that allows them to surface can begin the process of understanding them. As one comes into direct contact with these feelings and behaviors, one can begin to see the roots of them, their cause at the deepest level. Real freedom, which is the intention of Take Nami Do, comes only when one allows these feelings to surface, unearthing the core of the conflict. No matter how many skills are learned, if one doesn't allow this to happen, then one is only reinforcing the old patterns of destructive behavior. Practice itself becomes a means of reinforcing a pattern. The intention of Take Nami Do is to free the student to bring about intelligence in one's daily life, for Take Nami Do and life are one and the same.

"The young man was approached by the Old Warrior. 'What will you do to get away from my power?' asked the Warrior. 'Nothing,' replied the young man."

What joy,
playing with the form!
. . .just for the love of doing it.

The fundamental problem in relationship is the compulsive nature of violence. Can we use the structure of Karate as a mirror to understand violence? Without understanding violence fundamentally, we will only compound it.

Is there a root cause to violence? How and where do we begin to look for it? Is there a starting place for one's inquiry that will create an understanding of both individual and collective violence, so that one person's understanding can have an effect on the total?

As a starting point we will offer the working hypothesis that the core of the problem of psychological and hence sociological conflict is the construct of a separate entity called the self, I, ego, or thinker. This entity created by thought is a basic division within the psyche separated from the rest of thoughts. The fundamental cause of conflict in relationship, both individually and collectively, emanates from this internal division between the thinker, as "I" and thoughts or "they," manifested outwardly as conflict between us and them, the Russians and the Americans, the Arabs and the Jews, the good guy and the bad guy, the hero and the villain, God and the Devil. And each side thinks it is right.

"How does this divisive state come about?" This question is not intellectual; intellectual questions seek only intellectual answers. What we are doing is asking questions that will stimulate inquiry, that ability to observe what is actually happening.

The "how" in the question "How does this come about?" does not imply a method, an explanation, a means to get somewhere. A method implies time; observation is in the moment and therefore timeless. What this is asking is "Can we actually see what the causes are, now, each moment, and in so doing, end them?" So the "how" is a mirror of reality and not a method of accomplishment.

Seeing the danger of methods, can we now look to see what is happening to cause this basic division within the psyche, which is the root of psychological disorder, the source of individual and collective violence? Let's ask another question, "Does this ego self come about through fear, through the mind's reaction to death?"

As we now move into looking at the causes of conflict, can we be aware of our approach to this problem? We must be cautious along the way, because there are many dangers. One danger is approaching the problem with our preconceived notions, our prejudices. Can we suspend our views of what we think the problem is and look afresh? The nature of inquiry is this ability to suspend views and images and to look anew each moment. As we said, inquiry is observation, which is always in the moment, seeing the truth of what is occurring. It is learning without accumulation, it is learning that is immediate, direct, and without time.

Can we look at the question, "Does this ego self, which is the root cause of conflict, come about through fear, through the mind's reaction to death?" and actually look at the mind to see the truth or falseness of it? For it is the mind, each individual mind, which is the source of understanding. All we have to do is to be alert, to watch the mind in action or reaction, to see if this question is true or not.

What is death? Have we ever come face to face with death? Is there a realization of death that is actual and not theoretical? What do we know about death? Where do we get our ideas about death? Isn't death the unknown? If death is the unknown, what is there to fear? Isn't fear the known, the ideas and images we have about death?

It seems that the mind, not being able to meet the actuality of death, develops a construct about it, an image of what one thinks it is. These images come from the particular cultural influences and superstition built up over the years. Death therefore becomes intellectual, an abstraction. This image of death is fear, whether one is afraid of dying or feels the illusion of relief based on the belief in the afterlife, which is just another form of fear called hope or faith.

This image of death is based on the fear of not being, of not existing. The image can also represent the fear of pain through prolonged illness or by an accident. But it is not the fear of death, it is rather the fear of dying, the projected pain and suffering of it all.

Based on the fear of death—the image created by thought—the mind develops a defense against what we think death is. In other words, we don't want to think about death so we find ways to avoid or suppress it. If we look closely we can see that this defense creates a basic split in the process of thinking between the thought of death (fear), what we believe death is, and the entity, or self, the me, "I," or thinker who needs to control these fearful thoughts. It is this separation, this division, that we perceive as the source of conflict.

This division is caused in part by our believing that the thoughts of death are real, and not just thoughts. We don't see the fact that the brain has constructed these images of death and that we have taken the image, the thought, for the real thing. What is actually the truth is that thought, which is the known, cannot understand death which is the unknown. Since we don't see the truth of this, the problem becomes compounded in that we think we need to defend ourselves from (the fear of) death, from being nothing.

The me or self separate from the thoughts of death is created to control or do away with this fear. This separation and therefore the need to control or get rid of (the fear of) death becomes a battle, a struggle to overcome death and prolong life, as we know it, indefinitely. What we really want to prolong is me, the self.

One form of defense is to create a lifestyle that avoids this confrontation. Escapism comes in many forms. Religion, with its belief in the hereafter, is the greatest escape and perhaps the most dangerous because it creates the additional violence of becoming what we are not, of trying to live according to the ideal. What we call religion is too often a means of trickery in that we project the self into "God," so it can, by association, live life everlastingly.

In Japan, traditional Karate and the Martial Arts have been used as an escape from death, as a way to actually maintain the self. Many would disagree with this and say that the opposite is true, that is, the Martial Arts have been traditionally practiced as a way to face death. But if we look closely we can see that the essential ingredient in Karate and the Martial Arts is control, to control and discipline the self, to overcome fear. But this need to overcome the self, to overcome fear, is fear itself. Fear cannot overcome fear.

If one looks carefully at traditional Karate one can see this control in the constant repetition of form. Traditional Japanese Karate is based on Zen Buddhism. The essence of Zen is control. The student of Zen is exhorted to keep sitting, no matter what happens—just keep sitting. This sitting, called zazen, is a form of meditation whose subtle motivation is to attain enlightenment, that egoless, selfless, blissful state. But here again we have our dilemma—the self separate from thought, the self battling itself.

There is an old story: "One day a man was walking by a river when he saw two monks sitting quietly in a meditation position. He approached the monks and asked politely what they were doing. They replied that they were sitting zazen (a form of sitting meditation used in Soto zen). He asked why they were doing this and they responded that they were sitting to become enlightened. The man, on hearing this answer, sat down a short distance away from these two meditating monks. He picked up two rocks and began rubbing them together, to the annoyance of the monks. Finally when the monks could no longer stand this inter-ruption of their meditation, one asked what the man was doing. He replied, "I am trying to make a mirror by rubbing these two stones together." The monks exclaimed, "Sir, it is impossible to make a mirror by rubbing stones together!" "Likewise, it is also impossible to attain enlightenment by sitting!" replied the man.

Who is it that is trying to overcome the self? Isn't it the self?

If we have been observing our own minds (the mind) we have seen that a separation occurs psychologically, as the self or thinker and thoughts—in this case, the thoughts (fear) of death. This separation can be looked at as the struggle between the controller and the controlled. Thinking itself different from the fear, the controller (thinker, self, me or I) acts to *do* something to end this fear. As we have said, this reaction can be a form of escape, which is control, to get rid of it, or escape into the pursuit of ideals, of identifying ourselves with the eternal, with God. This pursuit is an escape from the actual, from the fact. The ideal, which is an escape, is an illusion. The fear of fear is the actual. One needs a sharp mind to cut through this fundamental illusion of the self; for if we don't cut through it, it will cut and kill us.

The fear of death builds up a resistance to looking, to life, which ends up killing us by closing us down psychologically. Resistance as a defense is the slayer of life.

The reaction to the fear of death becomes a battle, a struggle for dominance, of the self overcoming death. This battle has become romantically personified in many forms, depending on cultural conditioning. Religiously in the West, it generally takes the form of Christ promising eternal life if we overcome the Devil, or evil within us. The Crusades were a collective manifestation of this desire for the eternal good. In the East, generally it has become the quest for Enlightenment, of overcoming the self through a disciplined rote practice. Buddhism, especially Zen Buddhism, has become the source for this quest.

The greater the fear, the greater the need to overcome the fear, hence the greater reinforcement of the self, the controller. This vicious circle produces frustration and great tension due to the force of energy given to overcome or battle the fear of death, of annihilation.

This self becomes identified as a Warrior, the Good Guy (God), the Hero, who, by the sheer brute force of its individual will power, will destroy the forces of Evil (Devil), the villain or the Bad Guy. This internal struggle has been projected outwardly, as the Good Guys versus the Bad Guys. Whole nations depict the other side as demonic, the enemy to be overcome, slain. Can we see that this outward manifestation of conflict is the projection of the battle within in the form of the division between the thinker and thoughts, the controller and the controlled?

This internal dilemma projected outwardly can be seen in many cultural myths. These myths have been popularized in the current sagas of Martial Arts heroes, the independent, stoic, violent John Wayne type of individual, who alone will battle the forces of darkness. At present, in the mania of Martial Arts movies, magazines and books, we have the same "heroes." Bruce Lee, Chuck Norris and the fictitious Rambo all fulfill our repressed need to be a hero, to identify with the lone wolf tough guy. And now women have their counterparts in the films and magazines. The tragedy is that grown men and women are playing very dangerous children's games.

As we have seen, at the core of this fear of death is a conviction, a belief in the reality of these thoughts. We have seen that these unquestioned fears or beliefs have developed a defense against the fears and that this defense is manifested in the form of a self, an ego, or controller whose job it is to control and overcome these fears. This entity that is supposed to overcome the fear is "me," who by the effort of will-power, battles the fear and like the proverbial warrior of old, conquers it. But the tragic irony in this process is the mistaken notion that these thoughts about death are real, are actually death and therefore something to be afraid of and in need of conquering through the effort of a controlling self.

Not only are the thoughts of death not real but the separate self is also not real in that thought cannot divide itself. What is actually happening is that the self is fighting itself. The self is actually that which it battles, it is the fear itself; they are one and the same. In other words, the self is not different from that which it wants to control, to conquer. So all along thought was battling thought under the misguided notion that it could do something about fear. This self is the fear. There is only fear. There is no entity capable of conquering fear, no entity separate from the fear.

The fear of death and the entity that wants to end it are one and the same. Realizing that there is no divided self capable of battling (the fear of) death, leads to a fundamental understanding of the problem. When one sees that they are one and the same, that the need to control the fear of death is fear, is the self, then the whole thing begins to fall apart. When there is no separate I, or self, to control fear, then the fear ends because the self has no independent reality. In other words, when the separate I ends the fear ends, because they are one and the same and therefore there is no death as we know it. The confusion is created when we think that the thoughts of death are the real thing and when we then think we need to create the controller to overcome (the fear of) death.

The harder one tries (as the controller/self) to overcome the fear of death, the greater is the division and hence the greater is the conflict. It is like the Chinese finger puzzle: the fingers are inserted into each end of the wicker tube; when we want to remove our fingers, we try to pull them out. As we do, the puzzle tightens around our fingers. The harder we try to free ourselves the more the knot tightens. There is an analogy being made here between this puzzle and the way thought or the self works. The harder the self tries to control itself, to rid itself of the fear, which is itself, the greater is the fear. The realization that nothing is happening or even worse, that the fear is getting greater, the more one tries to get rid of it. The brain becomes locked into a futile and self-destructive battle of the self trying to end the self, or, in other words, thinking its way out of thinking.

Paradoxically the fear of the loss of control, loss of the self as the controller, becomes greater also. So the self becomes destructively reinforced in this self-defeating war within. The only outcome of this internal battle is either self-destruction or a hard, controlled self. Externally this battle is projected on the enemy; one struggles with other human beings for fear of being controlled.

The intention of Take Nami Do Karate is to bring this dilemma to the attention of the student. Without a fundamental understanding of the roots of conflict, learning Karate or any Martial Art will only reinforce and compound the problem, because that Martial Art will be used to wage war in the vicious circle of confusion.

This confusion in thinking is like a knot, as is tied in the Karate belt. This Karate belt knot is a square knot. When we pull hard on our belt, the knot gets tighter. The harder we pull, the tighter the knot. Metaphorically speaking, the knot represents the self as controller trying to control itself. The harder the self tries to control itself, the tighter the knot of confusion; it ends up finally strangling the life out of itself. Freedom comes when we become aware of this psychological knot. This awareness, because it understands, actually sees the dilemma, cuts through the knot, and in a single blow, frees us from its ever-tightening grasp.

Waiting without expectation the mind is still, open and unknowing.

PART II
A LESSON IN TAKE NAMI DO KARATE
THE FUNDAMENTAL PRINCIPLES

This section of the book will explore the essential aspects of the approach of this particular style. The principles explained here are to help the student understand Take Nami Do Karate as a practice that will aid him or her in understanding not only how to defend oneself, but far more importantly, help the student understand the larger context of the Art of Karate and its effects within everyday living.

A feeling of affection is vital for understanding oneself, for creating the right environment to explore the significance of "empty self" in the Art of Karate.

The Essence of Take Nami Do Karate

The unique emphasis of Take Nami Do, the Art of Karate, is its focus on empty self (Kara = empty), that is, on understanding and hence going beyond the psychological entity called the ego, the fundamental conflict this divisive state of consciousness brings about in relationship as the "I" versus the "you," the "we" versus the "they." In Take Nami Do the student is encouraged not only to understand what this self or ego structure is, how it comes into being, what effect it has on relationship, but to go beyond this psychological defensive mechanism and come into direct contact with one's biological defensive mechanism underlying this structure, with one's primitive, animalistic fight or flight reaction to being threatened.

One's fight or flight reaction is a reaction based on fear for survival. At one time in the course of human evolution it was called upon to protect the person from harm from predators. In some forms it is still necessary for survival. It has a place. Yet this primitive response has been carried over into the psychological realm causing unnecessary aggression which is manifested in competition, nationalism, and other forms of individual or collective antagonistic behavior.

In Take Nami Do the intention is to be free of this psychological reaction as the defensive structure called the self or ego. In order to be free of this the student needs to understand the nature and structure of the self in relationship and at the same time develop confidence through the learning of self-defense skills. When one has an intelligent understanding of the workings of the self and the confidence attained from learning to defend oneself physically (because the body can respond appropriately to a threat if it is necessary), then a threat does not immediately trigger this primitive psychological defense mechanism. A space is thereby created where one does not react psychologically, defensively. In this space there is the intelligence of inaction, a stillpoint where all reaction in time has ended. It is in this space that one is living without fear, free from the need to defend or attack psychologically. It is in this space that there is real peace. Physically you may have to defend yourself but inwardly you are free. If you have training in self-defense you are aware of the primitive response of fight or flight. You just notice it and act appropriately. But psychologically there is no reaction. So Take Nami Do, as the Art of Karate, intends to bring about an end to this deep-seated conflict, to empty self, through understanding the structure of the reactive pattern of the self and the underlying primitive response.

The form is not separate from oneself.
The form, when it emanates from genuine impulse is not from self-centeredness,
does not create conflict of self-expression.

The Art of Empty Self

"Scholars of old time said that the mind is originally empty, and only because of this can it respond (resonate) to natural things without prejudices (traces left behind to influence later vision). Only the empty mind can respond to the things of Nature. Though everything resonates with the mind, the mind should not remain in it. But once the mind has received (impressions of) natural things, they tend to remain and not to disappear, thus leaving traces in the mind. It should be like a river gorge with swans flying overhead; the river has no desire to retain the swan, yet the swan's passage is traced out by its shadow without any omission. Take another example. All things, whether beautiful or ugly, are reflected perfectly in a mirror; it never refuses to show anything, nor retain anything afterwards."

—Lin Ching-hsi

Empty self is not a romantic term. It is a metaphor for a mind that is not in reaction, a mind that is free of identification, of commitment psychologically. Empty self comes from understanding what fills the self up, not by forcibly trying to become empty. Becoming empty is the ideal and can therefore only cause violence in becoming what we are not. This concept of empty self is also called no mind. Empty self or no mind is a mind that is unconscious of itself; it is not disturbed by thoughts of fears and the constant challenges of the external environment. It is a mind that is not stuck. It is a free, flowing mind, likened to a stream of water. Thoughts come, thoughts go. This empty mindedness is not only used in the practice of Karate but applies to all activities in life. Self-consciousness impedes this flow causing an abrupt stop in consciousness. Thoughts of winning or losing, of gain or failure are all impediments because they are concerned with self, that psychological center point of reference.

The empty mind is the mind of the healthy person. It sees life clearly as it is rather than how it should be. This mind focuses on the activity and not the evaluation, therefore creating a nonjudgmental awareness of what is. In a practical way being empty, nonjudgmental, one concentrates on the task at hand and one does not get thrown off by thinking that creates fear. The practice of Karate with no-mind increases self-awareness and concentration, which also has benefits in one's daily life.

The moon shines on a still lake. There is no thing,
no discrimination of this or that, the scene is
untouched, pristine. Ducks land upon the lake,
ruffling the water for a moment and yet there is no
disturbance, the stillness remains intact, unaltered by
their sudden movement. There is nothing alien to
that moment, all is included and hence there is no
fear. . . no thing to defend against.

Basics

In traditional Karate the basics are the repetitive practice of self-defense techniques. Each time we practice we do basics: blocking, punching, kicking, and striking. We do these movements individually or in combinations of techniques. This repetitive practice of basics is necessary for perfecting technique as a person playing the piano needs to practice scales. Practicing basics also gives us the opportunity to focus our attention on each separate movement. This focusing allows the mind to concentrate on the task at hand, without wandering from the immediate moment. Practicing basics therefore can increase self-awareness. The basics are straightforward, relatively uncomplicated, technical moves that allow us the leisure to practice them simply and with care. They also allow us to experience **One Encounter—One Chance** in that each time we have only one opportunity to act with resolution.

The basics also mean something far deeper than technique. The rote practice of technique, by the sheer concentration on repetitive movements, can bring us temporarily to that stillpoint outside of time. The mistake many people make after experiencing this phenomenon is that the practice of basics— or other more complicated techniques— becomes the "how," the method to relive that experience, to capture that state. This is a great mistake.

The basics here refer to that unspoiled, positive state of livingness that is not of thought. If we look at a vase, for example, we see a vase, we see the object and the projected image of that object, the vase. The image comes from our experience, the past. We know what a vase is: it is to put flowers in. But seeing a vase without the image, the label, we see the real thing: the undifferentiated something that is not known, that is not of time. Thought is time: the past, present and future. The image has been made through time, experience, and is stored in the memory as the image of vase. This information is used for convenience. It is

52

necessary at certain times. It has a place. But what has happened is that the brain has collected psychological experiences—such as hurt, anger, and fear—images we have about ourselves and others, images as beliefs about life, what it should or should not be. For the most part we live in images, in thought, rarely ever touching the basics of life, that innocent, timeless quality that is creativity.

When we talk about understanding the basics in Take Nami Do Karate we talk not only about self-defense technique, which has a place in the larger context of the Art, but we also talk about the real basics of Karate, the inability to live in the now, outside of thought. Our practice of basics then refers to understanding why the brain has stored this psychological information as the me, the you, the hurt, the fear, the anger. When we talk about basics we understand that we mean finding out, through direct observation of thought itself, what prevents us from living in that alive state, that state from which passion arises. We understand that if we live in hurt and fear and anger (resentment) that we destroy relationship. Relationship based on the past is dead. If we relate to our husband, wife, children, friends through our images of them, then our relationships will be based on conflict because each person has an image of the other, and each person is either trying to have the other conform to their image or is rejecting change in the other person for the same reason.

Understanding the basics in Take Nami Do Karate has serious, far-reaching implications, not only individually but also collectively, not only in freeing oneself from conflict but also ending collective conflict, for the same root of discontent lies in both.

*The basic movements in Karate are the
foundation of the Art for they are the
earth and rock upon which we stand. We
do not practice them out of fear in the need
to defend ourselves. They are practiced for
their intrinsic beauty, for the dignity and
grace of the body's movement with spirit.*

Self-Defense

We train in self-defense through fix style, free style and even kata. We also train in self-defense in very practical ways such as, "What if he came up from behind and began to choke me?". This is a necessary yet very sad request for help. I am pained when I am asked to show people what to do in such and such a situation. It makes me sick to show someone how to hurt another. One day in class I showed the students a very violent technique, of bringing the elbow down on the back of the head while pulling the head forward by the hair with my free hand. I wanted us to face the realization of self-defense. A young woman burst into tears and ran out of the dojo. I felt like crying too. I am not calloused enough to not feel the terrible pain this realization must have caused that young woman.

I have agonized for years over the violence of Karate. I have given it up at times when I felt that all it was doing was creating more violence. Yet I keep coming back hoping to find more intelligent ways to cope nonviolently with hostile aggression. I have found that learning self-defense skills are not the answer. I tell the students to put the thought of self-defense out of their mind and just practice form. Perhaps this is a subtle way around the issue. I don't think so, for I find that if I practice form alone I am not reinforcing the fear that is the basis of learning a self-defense. I find that when fear is lessened the need to react out of fear is likewise lessened. If another senses that lack of fear in me I think this has a deterring effect on whether he or she will attack me. Fear generates more fear. People attack out of fear. When we have confidence I think that confidence is expressed to others and can help us in all sorts of conflict situations.

I still teach self-defense but I try to offer it in a more humane way (which is talked about in the section on Take Nami Do and Young People). There are so many ways to cope with conflict without resorting to physical aggression. I feel it is vitally important to learn about them, to practice them in the dojo, especially with young people.

Now when I show self-defense I always say that it is the last alternative we should use after we've exhausted all other avenues. We are all too human and in retrospect we wish we could have done better. We are violent people. I know I am. But what makes all the difference is our intention to end this violence. This intention is the Art of Karate, the heart of it.

The child has the capacity to understand the need to bring into limits the impulses of aggression. In so doing, he or she is allowed to explore him- or herself without the fear of losing control.

*It is the intention of the Art of Karate
to help students learn to defend themselves
so they don't have to.*

Fix Style

Fix style is when two or more people practice a prearranged attack/defense form of self-defense. All technique is known ahead of time. It is an excellent opportunity to practice the ability to defend against aggression. It is a highly controlled endeavor that allows the participants to exercise their particular degree of proficiency. It is a time when we can safely engage in a simulated fight.

Fix style not only allows for the perfection of self-defense skills but for the execution of what is called "One punch death blow." "One punch death blow" means just that. If one made contact at that point the technique would be lethal.

It is not our intent in Take Nami Do Karate to teach people how to kill! On the contrary we are interested in peace. But this is where the paradox comes in. In order to bring about peace one must come into direct contact with violence. This is another form of the paradox in that when one wants to come into contact with life, one must face death.

"One punch death blow" leads the student into the realm of the fine balance of life and death, outside of his or her conditioned defensive stance, his or her isolation of protective self-interest. "One punch death blow" is best practiced in fix style because fix style is the safest and most controlled self-defense training with a partner. Both Kata and Basics are more solitary, individual endeavors that do not bring the student into the reality of death. Practicing "one punch death blow" in fix style dispels the frozen illusion of our images of death by allowing us actually to run the razor's edge of death. In the contact with that precipice, one cannot help experiencing his or her vulnerability, that tenuous, fragile hold on life. In this contact with a partner there is a real understanding and humility. We can kill and be killed. Our heroic, romantic images of the Warrior fade quickly. Through "one punch death blow," we are aware of the precious time allowed us to enjoy this fleeting moment, this fleeting phenomenon called life. This realization has an effect on our relationships to other human beings. It opens our eyes and lets us see that we are all vulnerable, that we will all die soon enough.

Can there be a non-competitive relationship when engaging in the combative aspects of Karate? Real learning occurs when each person challenges the strengths and weaknesses in the other in a manner of mutual cooperation. In this way, each person must help the other to be strong, but one does not need to overpower the other in so doing.

Free style

Free style is when two or more people test their self-defense skills in spontaneous, free-form action. There are limitations imposed upon these contestants by a referee and judges. There is the rule of no contact in Take Nami Do Karate and gentlemanly considerations of fair play prevail. It is not street fighting; it is not chaos. It is a highly structured, excellent form of skill in action.

The student not only receives valuable training in self-defense but also develops a heightened sense of awareness. In free style the students are allowed to attack and defend with tremendous intensity, stopping just short of impact when delivering a technique. This high-speed, intense exchange of techniques puts one on the edge of the sword. Any miscalculation, any momentary lapse of attention could bring serious injury, and death.

In free style the student gives everything and in so doing, goes beyond him or herself. It is this going beyond the self that brings one to the beauty of Karate. Beauty is not in the eye, in the image of what we think is beautiful. This is comparison. Beauty comes when the "me" is not. It comes when, for a moment, we enter that stillpoint of un-self-conciousness beyond time, when we enter timelessness, the moment itself. Oh, that wonderful feeling of not being, the beauty of it!

Kata

Kata is form. It is a set of prearranged movements, a routine one practices in order to become proficient in the self-defense aspect of Karate. In this way, Kata is a set or customary order of doing something, it is a structure or pattern one follows to attain a result. Therefore, Kata as form is a formality molded by instruction and discipline. Yet form moves beyond defense, beyond result and formality. When one first practices Kata it is mechanical, as is necessary in order to learn technique properly. After practicing Kata for a time, one brings forth spirit, the energy generated from contacting the essence of the Kata, that movement that is not of time. The beauty of the movement is then for itself alone. In form with spirit there is dignity and gracefulness in the gesture. There is a majestic quality to movement when one's spirit is complete. In this, one gives one's total attention to that form, to live in the world with one's own body, here and now. Then, form and Kata are one and the same, and that form is in everything one does. Kata becomes complete action and the form pervades all activity. Kata becomes ethics, it becomes conduct, it is how one behaves. It is the intention towards right behavior. Form as Kata puts that which is, in order. It gives shape and order to how one acts in the world.

Oh, that freedom of spirit,
breaking the bonds of one's inhibitions,
to suddenly leap up and out of the confines of self-control
...and yet to remain within the limits of intelligent discipline.

How beautiful is the form when one is free of images of what it should be. One's positions are reflections of the elemental world, the world of nature. In this there is no division as the "me" and the "not me."

Kiai

In Karate we *kiai*, which is a type of yell or shout. This shout does two things. First, the expelling of air through the mouth in a strong, vibrant manner gives focus to the Karate movement or technique by making it stronger. This happens because the abdominal muscles contract and discharge extra power. The kiai also has the effect of psychologically disarming a potential assailant; the tremendous energy generated by the kiai can shake the assailant's intention to do harm, for it temporarily disorients him. It can also reach deeply into the person and make contact in a fundamental way beyond words or visible intentions; the kiai can bring the person back to his or her senses, back from the depths of fear and hurt to the clear and untainted moment. This can be a very shocking thing, especially when it occurs suddenly. It is like being doused with cold water when you are asleep. It brings you out of your dream world into the blazing daylight of reality. This sudden awakening from one's nightmare into the moment is the intention of the Art of Karate. Sustaining that state is another matter, and must be approached in a different manner.

Also, Kiai simply means energy and union, as in Aiki(do). Unifying energy means to bring an end to conflict. When conflict is absent, then naturally there is harmony, there is a state of unified energy. The lack of harmony or discord conversely means a state of fragmented energy, a divided state. When one is intending to act out of fear, hurt and anger, then one is out of harmony with things as they are, for these qualities are born of the mind when there is a state of conflict. Being free of the disorder of fearful thinking, one is undivided, not isolated from living. When one kiais, then one is not only focusing energy for more power or psychologically to disarm an assailant; the kiai has a much more far-reaching effect— it affects the whole balance of nature. So when you kiai, what are you doing? Where does this energy generate from in you? If it is out of fear,

72

which just adds more conflict, it is not a kiai but a scream or shriek. A kiai is a mightier shout, an expression of the union of energy within and without. One's actions are always in accordance with nature's harmony, even in defending oneself. There is no conflict. There is only the appropriate response to the moment and the great undivided force of energy meeting that response.

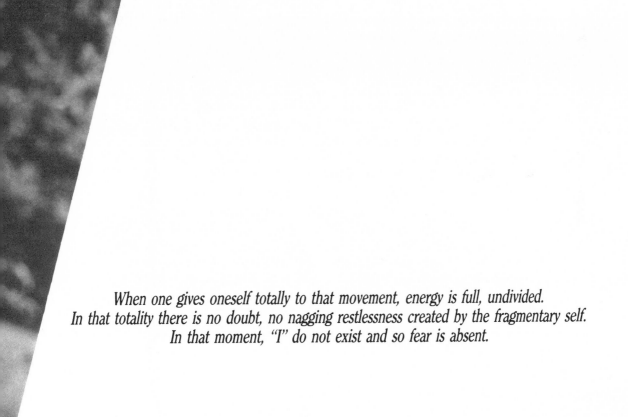

When one gives oneself totally to that movement, energy is full, undivided.
In that totality there is no doubt, no nagging restlessness created by the fragmentary self.
In that moment, "I" do not exist and so fear is absent.

Attitude

There is a formula in Take Nami Do Karate: Attitude and form equals speed and power. The foundation of this formula is attitude. If one has understood attitude, the form (of Karate) is free to express itself. If we concentrate our energies on form then speed comes of itself. Add this together and it equals power. Power is not usually available at the beginning; it is missing until one has understood the nature and structure of attitude. Wanting power is merely the superficial development of an attitude and therefore prevents power.

Many people merely want some sort of recognition from Karate, like the Black Belt. This typifies the incorrect attitude. Some people want to be able to fight, or compete, or want to gain power over others through Karate. Others want to impress, to show off their knowledge. These attitudes are all based on the need to be someone, to become something which is based on fear and therefore are destructive. Attitudes of this sort are forms of judgment, of comparison.

Then there are those who love the movements in Karate, enjoy the energy they receive as a by-product of the physical training. They understand that Karate is serious, an endeavor that brings them into direct confrontation with themselves. This is the correct attitude only if it comes naturally, without thought of personal gain. When one loves what one does, then the shell of self-centered attitudes we all have falls by the wayside, and attitude ceases to be a problem. When we understand our attitude, our beliefs about life, ones that have been conditioned into us from birth, then we begin to be free of them and our practice of Karate becomes meaningful.

Focus

Focus is the concentration of energy at a single point for an instant. Focus can be demonstrated in a Karate technique such as a punch where the power of the mind/body is brought into play at the target. Focus in Karate is like snapping a wet towel, the force comes at that point of contact of the furthest extension of the towel just before it becomes a limp rag.

But focus in the Art of Karate is more than the power generated in a self-defense technique. It is the ability to be continuously aware of the minute and subtle movements of thought. For it is thought that motivates behavior, that generates the destructive patterns of belief, that sustains the idealized image of becoming, that isolates the self from experience, that creates war, poverty and ignorance. Focusing on the potential for destructive behavior based on conditioned thinking takes a great deal of energy, for this focused awareness cannot be relaxed for a moment. It is like living under the double-edged sword. Be inattentive for a moment and we are cut by the reactions of fear and psychological survival.

Focus means coming into the moment, staying with the facts and not moving away into the wishful thinking of ideals. If we drift off that focused attention we will immediately become aware of it and in so doing will bring ourselves back to the fact, to reality.

In our practice of Karate techniques we must give our focused attention to each and every movement, not moving away into thoughts of accomplishment, pride, or self-conscious comparison.

When one is focused, there is an intense alertness. This is not the narrowness of concentration which emanates from a motive to look. Focus is meeting the vital challenge of the real world; it is being wide awake to the moment because the moment demands it!

Spirit

What is spirit? The word "spirituality" is also used. The expressions, "breaking one's spirit" or "freeing the spirit" are common. Can we substitute the word "passion" for "spirit?" Passion does not mean lust; it means finding great energy in doing what we love to do.

Have you noticed that people lack spirit or passion? They have a great deal of energy but that energy is frenetic; its motivation comes from anxiety, from keeping up with the competition. This energy is not passion. It is destructive. Real spirit or passion is creative. It is discovering anew what life offers, if one is serious, open. Why don't we have spirit, passion? What prevents it? For one trying to get spirit sets spirit up as a goal, an ideal, which causes conflict. Perhaps understanding what prevents spirit we can eliminate what it is not. By understanding what is not real passion we may be able to discover our neglected passion within.

In our practice of Karate do we have spirit? Or are we just mechanically going through the movements in the hopes that Karate will somehow magically solve our problems? Motivation out of fear, out of hope can generate a great deal of energy but this is not real spirit, passion. Can we see the conditioned attitudes we have that prevent real spirit in our practice of Karate? Is our attitude based on the concern that having real passion in our movements is too violent, too aggressive, too uncontrollable, too scary, not proper (behavior), too masculine (not feminine), not humanistic (loving)? There are many people who have an attitude that Karate is too violent and that practicing Karate evokes more violence. This may be true if one practiced Karate as it is traditionally taught. But if one is serious, then the opposite is true. Those who are afraid of the violence in the Art of Karate and shun it for their ideals of nonviolence are paradoxically bringing about violence.

Real passion arises when there is a serious and

urgent intention to understand violence. Running away from violence through adherence to ideals, however noble, is violent. We need to come into direct contact with ourselves, with violence, to understand it. Conflict, shunning what we fear as violence, dissipates our spirit or energy to find out. We would rather feel secure and hide in some sort of belief system than face the fact of who we are. What prevents facing ourselves and our violence is judgment, condemnation. When we judge, we deny passion; when we condemn, we deny spirit. We build a wall of resistance around us as a defense to protect us from the pain and hurt of judgment. In facing the fact there is only that. There is pain in the condemnation, not in the truth. We develop an image out of defense that reassures us that we are not a horrible, bad, or violent person. This image is the ideal image, the opposite of being violent. This ideal image is in fact what we assume we should be; it is the mind's way of dealing with the fact of violence. But it doesn't work. It only creates more violence by denying fact and conforming to the ideal.

Since we have created a wall of resistance around us in the idealized image we have (that we are good people), is there anything we can do to break through this wall? (We have to be very careful when we think in terms of rightful doing because this usually means creating more ideals.) In practicing the physical self-defense techniques we can reduce the barrier of rigid resistance, giving ourselves totally to each movement. When we kiai, when we focus, when we punch that single punch we must do it with our total beings, as if our life depended on it. **One Encounter— One Chance** means just this! We need to give everything to burn through our resistances.

We also need to understand the nature of resistance, of what prevents spirit, passion. We can do this at any time by watching our minds, observing thought and how, when thought enters the psychological realm, it creates conflict. If we are to live intelligently, which is the intention of The Art of Karate, we need to understand all this. For a life without spirit, without passion, is death, the death of life.

Spirit is in allowing life to move within you.
This is so simple and natural, a child can do it.
But spirit is lost in our conditioned so-called civilized world of fear,
a world created through reaction to the awe of being nothing.

Mind Like Moon—Mind Like Water

As the moon shines equally on everything, so does the mind encompass all it perceives without discrimination. In Karate when one is freestyling, if there are thoughts of winning or losing, or what technique one should use, these thoughts are like clouds that pass in front of the moon blocking the light (of awareness). So too with mind like water. Still water reflects only what is there. Thoughts are like dropping pebbles into that water, causing ripples in the mind. The distracted mind cannot respond accurately and immediately to what is happening.

These concepts (mind like moon—mind like water) are important not only in the practice of Karate, in freestyling or self-defense, but are also important to one's everyday life. The challenges of living demand accurate and intelligent responses. When the mind is clouded or disturbed by waves of anxious thinking, then one's response is diminished and therefore one is not capable of meeting the challenge fully.

But there is more to these concepts. The word "mind" referred to in Japanese Karate means "consciousness," which is all of living. What we in the West refer to as "mind" is only a small part of this Japanese concept of mind. The typical Western notion of mind is the analytical, logical, intellect, a necessary tool for living, for creating science and technology. But "mind" in "mind like moon—mind like water" has a far deeper and more profound meaning. This mind is the foundation of all consciousness, it is consciousness aware of itself. This mind is in stillness, in silence. When the intellectual mind finds its proper place in living, in action, then this order can pave the way for the larger mind to enter.

It is this larger mind from which consciousness emanates. It is where all things arise and disappear into the void. It is the seat of being, the wellspring of life.

When there is a moment of forgetfulness, a stillpoint in the chaos of frenetic living, that mind may blossom. But all too often one is caught up in the smaller mind, in the frenzy of self-centered preservation, in trying to find psychological security. It is only by not knowing that one can come upon this mind. In not knowing there is intelligence. Not knowing does not mean ignorance, not thinking. Not knowing means that thought is not seeking security in itself.

Mind Like Moon— Mind Like Water is a metaphor for the mind that is intelligent, a mind that is sane.

There is no time to reflect on what is happening when there is danger. Confronted by fire, there is immediate action; meeting the anger of attack there is only the encounter. If one's attitude is of defense or self-preservation one will be cut by indecisiveness. So move in harmony with the challenge, not against it. In harmony there is the totality of relationship...in defense there is the fragmentation of "me" versus "you" in which both lose.

PART III
TALKS WITH STUDENTS

These talks were produced during a period of six years between 1980 and 1986 for the students in the Take Nami Do Northern California School.

Late one night I went for a walk around my small, cozy neighborhood. Outside, the overcast fog had rolled in and covered the town in a low-lying blanket of dark mist. Lights from the city eight miles away were muffled just beneath the edge of the fog. A dog was barking in the distance, a comforting and wonderfully lost sound in the night. I walked up my street very slowly. The wind passing through a tall, scruffy palm tree stopped my walking. There was a magic in that unknown movement. Wind chimes played an unfamiliar melody adding to the mystery of the night. I sat on a bench lost and unknowing, but I was home. There was nothing else. Only an occasional car jarred the dark night...searching, piercing eyes of light...then gone. I was alone.

In our practice, we bow. We bow at the door of the dojo, entering and leaving. We bow at the edge of the mat, also when entering and leaving. We bow to each other, standing and sitting. What is this bow really? Perhaps it is just a part of the unquestioned ritual, an Oriental custom, like a hand-shake. We also create the yoi position, the ready stance. What are we ready for when we do this? Have you ever thought about it?

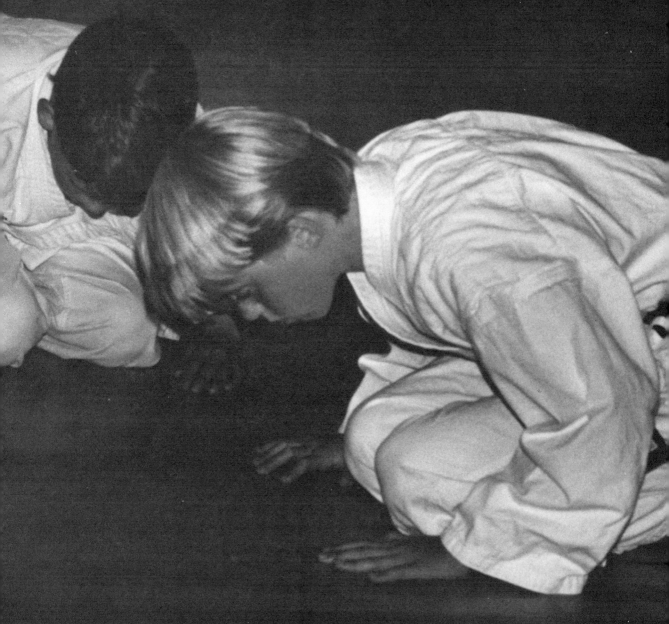

Is the bow just another meaningless ritual?

Or can it be a genuine gesture of respect
which means one puts aside self-concern for another?

It seems to me that the bow is the epitome of all Karate stances. When we bow we are paying respect to the dojo, practice area, and to one another. But a bow is more than this, for respect could become a mere habit, a custom practiced only repetitiously. I feel the bow is also paying respect to the moment, an acknowledgement of the grace of each now, of livingness itself. It is such a graceful move, hands at sides, feet together, arching body slowly forward, eyes down. Some say that the bow was originally intended to show humility and trust, for in bowing the person exposes the back of his or her neck to attack. But we are beyond that. Karate has moved beyond its origins when monks and Samurai were being attacked and attacking.

It is the expression of life, the attitude and state of mind that allows life to enter, that has no resistance or defenses to what it receives. It is a movement that expresses the openness of mind, the quality of spaciousness, vastness.

The yoi, or ready stance, in the Art of Karate, if practiced properly, becomes the single most significant stance, in that it expresses the mind/body that is alert, aware, attentive. There is no reason, no intention, no effort in this alertness. It expresses or rather — it _is_ — the alertness one sees in other animals. Have you ever watched a cat, how naturally and effortlessly alert it is? It is ready for whatever comes its way, without tension, without being on guard. This quality of the yoi stance is the natural ability of being alive, without the fearful mind entering. It is the eye of the storm, it is the eternal movement, endlessly attentive to itself.

When we bow, we just bow; when we take the yoi stance, there is just attention, just what is.

"Being really free, in theory as well as in actuality, not only in practice in the dojo, but also in one's everyday life — is the real meaning of Karate."

When I was around ten or eleven years old, I spent a summer at a resort town on the Atlantic Ocean. I remember vividly one incident that changed my life dramatically. It was the first time I came very close to death.

One day I was at the beach; I don't remember who was there, perhaps my parents or my aunt or uncle. I was playing in the ocean quite close to shore when a large wave surprized me from behind. I remember being knocked down and under the wave, being tumbled over and over, not knowing which way was up, out of breath, not being able to stand up in the strong tide and undercurrent. It happened so quickly! Suddenly I was pulled up by a stranger, a man, and stood, rather bewilderedly, at the shore's edge. I went back up to my blanket, not knowing how deeply shocked I really was. This experience had an effect on me for many years, both in dreams and in that I was afraid to go swimming in the ocean.

I used to dream of tidal waves. They would come up unexpectedly and I would try to run away. But I couldn't move fast enough, the sand was too soft for me to get my footing; so the wave would crash on me. This was a terrible feeling. It took me years to get over these dreams. They would occur once in a while, the same wave, being huge and terrifying, and it would crash on me. But one night, after a period of understanding in my life, this dream was suddenly different. Instead of the wave crashing over me, I stopped running and turned to face it. As I did, I dove right into the low part of its force and came up on the other side. It was at first terrifying, but then as I came out on the other side, it was exhilarating! Later, this dream occurred periodically with me diving into the wave. Then one night I had my last wave dream. That night I found myself surfing on the tip of the wave, moving with its force. What a wonderful feeling, so effortless and yet so powerful!

This story is an example of what Take Nami Do is. The literal translation from Japanese of TAKE is "bamboo," NAMI means "wave," and DO means "way." These symbols are metaphors of something important that I want to share with you.

In Karate, there is often mention of Eastern mysticism or spirituality. I find it usually vague, not really practical — that is, not usable in one's everyday living. Karate is full of Eastern philosophical symbols that give it a certain flavor or character. This appeals to many people, to their desire for something special, so they can feel special, different, important. It seems to fill them up, so to speak.

People also are interested in this notion of enlightenment — the freedom from suffering this purports to offer — and this appeals to people's need to be free of the problems they live each day, the boredom, the lack of real passion in their lives, real power to bring about change. So the spirituality or mysticism of Karate and the Martial Arts is a way for some to identify with an ideology outside themselves, in order to enhance the quality of living.

If Karate, or any of the Martial Arts, is to have an effect on people's lives, not just for a short time in the dojo, but all day, every day, then I think we must take it out of vague Eastern terms and really examine it intelligently to see if it can have a functional and practical use for us. Take Nami Do means the way of bamboo and wave, but what is meant by that — what is its practical application?

In Take Nami Do Karate, this symbol of bamboo represents yielding, or blending. It also represents conformity, not disciplined obeyance but rather "being in harmony with." This principle is seen both in the physical and the psychological realms. Physically TAKE (bamboo) represents the block or parry, the defensive, evasive technique. In defending with a block or parry, the student must actually work together with his or her opponent. This working together consists of moving with the attack, yielding to its

94

force so that both the attacker and the one attacked are not unnecessarily hurt in the process.

A proper block can be given with enough force to thwart the aggressor's intention to continue attacking. The defender can also redirect the attack by such evasive moves as ducking, bobbing, shifting, sliding, parrying and the like. Each maneuver is designed to bypass the force of the attack and thereby render it harmless. Proper blocking requires a keen sense of timing, control, and an overall alertness.

Psychologically, bamboo means yielding also. Suppose someone calls you a name, insults you. What do you do? How do you respond? Or, do you react? Do you get angry? Do you want to defend? Do you want to insult the person back? Why? What causes the reaction in you? Was it hurt that wanted to strike back? What is this hurt, where does it come from? Who is hurt? Can you see that these questions are important to ask? Not to answer intellectually, but to use the questions to actually look at what is happening! Can you see the difference? Can you also see the difference here between getting caught up in foreign-sounding words, Eastern religious terminology, getting ego-associated with these special words, and in asking serious, commonsense questions, in straightforward everyday language, questions that can lead to real understanding, and not affected behavior?

So TAKE means the ability to yield, to not resist physically or psychologically. Physically and practically this leads to quicker and more responsive actions, the ability to move immediately out of harm's way. Psychologically, it also means to not resist. If one is not resisting, whether it is an insult or even praise, then one can be aware of what is actually happening, one can learn from it. When you resist, there is no learning, just the pain of resistance.

NAMI means "wave." Wave here denotes, in physical terms, the movement of energy. It can be a counter-attack, or dispelling harmful aggression by turning the opponent's attack against him or her.

Psychologically the wave symbolizes the unconscious or

subconscious storehouse of reactions one has built up.
This subconscious storehouse, what it is, how it comes into
being, is one of the most important aspects of understanding the Art of Karate. In a person are stored up all the
unresolved hurts, all the anger, frustrations, the insults, all
the years of conditioned reactions to living, not only in one's
own life but the legacy of the culture one lives in. There is
also the psychological/genetic storehouse of the evolution-
ary lineage of mankind. All of that remains, charged in the
sub- or unconscious, just below the level of our daily con-
scious work-a-day world, dictating our lives, ready to pour
forth its contents, rather like a wave crashing on the shore.
Now this wave symbol is used in Karate only so you can be
reminded of what both impedes and propels force.

If you have seen that this unconscious wave of pent-up
reactions really exists and have seen, or observed how you
react in your life because of it, then you will begin to understand the need for and the nature of the bamboo, that is,
for being able not to resist this momentum of subconscious-
ness. You cannot resist it, suppress it. Resistance only sets
up more conflict, more violence. The subconscious reaction,
why it is able to play itself out, is the violence. You don't
want to add more violence by resisting that. But you also
don't want to let that wave crash on you.

You must learn to dive into the wave, that is, when you
see the reactions coming, the hurt, the anger, the desire to
strike out, you just watch, you do not resist, you do not
attack. You have begun to see that the way to understand,
and hence go beyond this wave-like momentum of violent
reactions, is to observe it, as if you were in the eye of a
storm. A space is created in which observation takes place.
This space is understanding, is intelligence. Instead of
reacting, you watch both the insult and your reaction, the
wave, all at once. You watch the whole movement without
interference, without acting upon it. This watching is this
space between your own reactions and yourself. Before you
were those reactions, you were caught up in their momentum, and the wave crashed. Now your response is from a

different plane or level of consciousness; you are not identified with and not committed to the momentum of your past reactions. You see that the real problem is not the subconscious, rather the real problem is one's identification with the subconscious. Therefore, understanding the nature of the wave, understanding the nature of the bamboo, you can understand and see the need for action that is not reaction, one that is free from the identification or commitment to one's subconscious charge. This understanding, at the moment of insult, or attack, is immediate. Understanding is action. Understanding is transformation.

This collection of subconscious reactions, the violence it is and creates, the violence of resisting it, of suppressing it, is called the self. It is the past experiences as memory, as the subconscious. It is also the thinker, the entity that tries to control this subconscious momentum, tries to control thought, which is itself. The word "Karate" means empty hands or more profoundly, empty self. We study the Art of Karate not to fill the self, not to inflate ourselves, not to puff up our egos because we need to defend. We study the Art of Karate because we experience spontaneously the need for an empty self, for being empty of this momentum, for being free of hurt, anger, defensiveness and aggression—that is, of violence itself. This is the foundation of one's practice here and everywhere. If one really understands this process, the way of Take Nami Do, the Art of Karate, of emptying self, then one can ride the tip of the wave.

Can thinking solve the problems thinking has created?
Sitting quietly can we observe the conflict inherent in this division and see
the impossibility of such a thing?

"In Karate we work in our practice to free the mind/ body from its dis-ease, so it can be flexible, supple, free- moving, so it can return to a state of harmony, balance and well-being."

I want to talk about what we call "exorcises" in Take Nami Do; to exorcise the demon of tension and aggression stored up in our minds and bodies. It seems that from birth we are bombarded with assaults on our psyches. These insults or assaults are registered as psychological hurts. They are stored up in us year after year, as we have talked about before. These psychological assaults are made by those around us, because they too were assaulted before us. These hurts come from another being upset and angry with us, because perhaps they are anxious, feeling the stresses of work and so on. Perhaps they come from others because they have an image of themselves and therefore the people around them. These images are the shoulds they live by, the oughts, the values, the code of behavior we call ethics or morality. In their need to conform to their image, their ideal personification of who they think they ought to be, their "good" selves, they put a great deal of pressure on themselves and others to conform as they do. They use a system of punishments and rewards to control behavior. One of the most powerful punishment/rewards they use is love. "I love you if..." is how it goes. What is implied, as the punishment, is that there is no love if you do not conform to their standards. Using love as a motivation for good behav- ior creates a split in the young person. The psychologist Carl Rogers called this "conditions of worth." Our worth is conditional, depending on how we act.

The one who decides to play this game is the child who decides to repress his or her own natural intelligent re- sponses to living, who affects good behavior, who conforms and becomes good, develops an image, a facade, a persona (from the word "personality"). From there on, anything that doesn't conform to that self-image doesn't fit and is immediately rejected. This process of conforming to an image, an ideal of goodness, rejecting all that which doesn't fit that ideal is a very painful process. It is full of conflict because that which does not fit according to the ideal is rejected, repressed, eliminated—but that which is rejected is a part of who we are.

The more we try to be good the more we have to eliminate that which is bad. This sets up a struggle within us between good and bad. (I am talking about the *process* of becoming good—the content of goodness, that is, kindness, gentleness, generosity, and truthfulness are obviously healthy qualities to live. What I am talking about here is how we arrive at these qualities.)

We grow up with the image and the hurts, tensions and struggles of living with being good according to the idealized image of goodness. These hurts are painful so we develop a defensive system to block out the hurt, just as we would block a kick or punch. Behind this wall of conformity and defense there is a building up of pressure. This pressure and defense starts to show itself in the way we act towards ourselves and others. Our actions become controlled, contrived, respectable. We begin not to listen to what others are saying, or what our own minds may be telling us about our condition. This not listening becomes a deadening process.

These hurts and defense against the hurts become manifested in the body. This has been called "body armor" by the psychoanalyst Wilhelm Reich. It shows up as physical tension in certain areas of the body, such as a jutting forward of the neck, head and chin ("take it on the chin"), the rounding, forward movement of the shoulders and the thickening of the neck muscles ("bull neck" and "red neck" caused by constriction of the blood vessels). The chest that becomes either overly extended or sunken in, and rigidity of the general movement of the body while moving are all characteristics of body armoring. This dis-ease is a problem that has come about, on one level, by not understanding the original process of image-making, of living according to ideals. In Karate, no matter how much technique you have,

101

body armor undermines it.

In our practice we must do exorcising: exercises that aid in this recovery, aid in releasing pent up anger, hurt, frustration, tension, stress. In order to accomplish this we must first have an environment in the dojo that is safe, trusting, caring. When we feel a safeness, we can begin to work out this stored aggression that has become a lifestyle, through competition, through proving ourselves.

Some ways we can begin to free ourselves from these self-imposed restrictions are through training in the Karate basics, through a rigorous, disciplined, spirited, intense practice of the forms. This physical endeavor begins to allow us to act out the defensiveness in a most vigorous fashion. It aids in working through the many blocked up bodily areas. Physical working out has, also, a cathartic or releasing effect on the mind. As we work on the basics, we at first strike out in violent gestures in an awkward outflowing of inner feelings. After a while these violent and awkward gestures are slowly transformed into artful movements, movements that are graceful, beautiful.

This change from awkward gestures to artful movements is therapeutic, curative, in that as we are able to reduce the need for defending, we have reduced the quantity of stored tension and stress by reducing our body armor. Therefore, this exorcising is healthful. It is a chance for the mind/body to right itself, to regain flexibility and subtleness. Then, perhaps, we have laid the right foundation for something deeper to happen.

Without asking or trying we may experience a sense of freedom that is the goal of the Art of Karate. Call that quality what you will, for the word is not the thing. It is what we are seeking, whether we are aware of it or not. But we must first understand the need to exorcise, the need to safely release pent-up stored defensiveness, aggression, tension and stress.

A mind/body that is in a state of dis-ease, tense, angry, frustrated, defensive, is a mind/body that is unhealthy. We cannot go beyond our condition to receive anything unless, through diligent practice and understanding, we work this through.

"If the Art of Karate is meaningful, it must be lived as a way of life, not practiced by rote, by habit, through ideals."

Sometimes when I walk out in the garden and flowers around my cottage, I see these minute silvery trails and I know that snails have moved about in the night. Have we ever watched a snail for awhile? Do we have the patience to watch a snail? How very slowly it moves. I find it hard to stay there, my mind wants to go. It's chomping at the bit, anxious, being its usual monkey mind. At times I can just watch the snail and also just watch the mind (myself) jumping around. It is an interesting juxtaposition.

It is a wonder how delicate living is, how the day turns almost imperceptibly into night and how the night so gently, slowly, subtly gives way to dawn, an interfusing of light and shadow, a fragile continuous movement. To be able to experience that subtle, that frail and delicate and yet powerful movement is to experience the quality of life. It seems to me that most of us are living in measured success, in results. Yet life itself is not appreciated in quantity, in the results one gains through concentration of effort. This has some place in living, but they are fleeting experiences. Life itself is process, the moment-to-moment heightened sensitivity of what is.

I remember once being with a group of children on a nature walk. I had my hand lens (a magnifying glass) around my neck on a piece of cord. In the spring grasses there were many wildflowers. I bent down low on the ground and with my hand lens looked down into a small delicate white flower. There was a bright yellow inside, much too wondrous to put into words. Then I noticed a very small spider resting on a drop of dew on the side of the flower. What a sight, this miniature world, this incredible microcosm! The bright yellow and black spider on a crystal clear droplet of dew! All for free! Just there, not asking to be looked at. I thought, "How many other incredible worlds do I miss each day, each moment?" All this wonder—and my mind is so busy with getting, becoming, being something, someone. All that tremendous, anxious effort to be, to get and the violence of all that! Here I was, looking at "heaven in a wildflower," as the poet Blake wrote.

I remember subsequently walking around my neighborhood and experiencing all the seemingly hidden worlds. A particular bush of honeysuckle, grabbed my attention with its incredible odor when I passed by. When I leaned forward toward that bush, closed my eyes, and breathed in that scent of honeysuckle, there was only nameless essence—there was no one there smelling that flower! It was a complete, timeless peace, bliss (if I may use that word), and yet at the same time it was nothing at all. The simple act of smelling that flower, on a busy street, with life going on all around, for that one delicate, timeless, unspeakable moment—is all I have been searching for. I know this deeply inside. It is so common, so simple, and so right; the ordinary becomes the extraordinary. It is there all the time, if we can just experience it. But bliss is not so easy to maintain, for immediately afterward, I tried to smell another flower. The scent was hardly there. When I intentionally approached a bush for an experience, it didn't seem to happen. Only when I came across it accidentally did it reach out to me.

I cannot approach it. Why are we always trying to get from life, to manipulate and control it, instead of being open to letting it give to us? In Karate practice when the form moves us, when we go beyond the self-conscious repetitious training, and touch that timeless quality of living, why does the mind hold on to that and try to recapture it again in the next form?

When we practice Karate we can so easily become goal-oriented, so product-fixated (the goal being power, prestige, or some vague desire for enlightenment or whatever name we give it). Our moves are so intentional, so hard, so quick. Can we practice our movements like the snail, but with intention, unintentionally? Can we practice our form like the snail? Just watch our monkey mind, see how it wants to get finished, to move on. Watch how it is so unhappy with this moment, how it is wanting to be done, to be on to the next thing. Have we ever slowed down to watch how we eat? How, while we are chewing food, tasting the flavor, the mind is already on the next bite, or on dessert? This anxious mind reminds me of a carrot tied on a string dangling from a stick that has been placed out in front of a horse, just far enough so that the horse keeps moving forward trying to get it. Do we see this analogy in ourselves? As we practice our movements be aware of this. Also watch, or feel, what it feels like to move like a snail. Feel how the muscles move, each subtle movement from one position to the next, feel the fine tuning the body possesses naturally when we are aware of it, when our minds are not anxiously pushing the body beyond itself. Feel this, be aware of these minute changes and we will find out how joyful it can be.

Our performance in Karate, our form, will develop faster if we do it really slowly, for then the mind/body can see all the mistakes, the little errors, and can correct them simultaneously. It is important to make these mistakes because that is the act of learning; making mistakes is the experimenting, the testing out of what we are doing.

Feel very free to make many mistakes. I would like to encourage you to make mistakes, but I would ask you to make them slowly enough so you really see them. When we do our Karate movements — our basics and katas — too quickly, we cannot see our mistakes. Then someone tells us, points them out to us, and we think about them, we try to understand them through our mind, in thoughts, but we do not actually see them. These thoughts become our "shoulds" and therefore we begin to set up an ideal image of what is proper form. We try to become this image, to conform to the image, the "shoulds," and we begin to paralyze ourselves.

Can we do our movements like the snail and follow our minds, just watch, aware of our movements, feeling the pleasure and health of a body moving with slow grace? Just slow down, look, and listen. Maybe this attention will show us more of who we are, what makes us work, how we keep ourselves anxious, speedy. If we can begin in our Karate practice to slow down, enjoy the form and watch, this will have an effect on the whole of our life, the life we live all day, outside the dojo.

Is there really a separation as "you" and "me?"

The sounding of a bell...the ring permeates
and fills the space between us and we are
gone...and there is nothing.

So who is the enemy?

"If meditation is supposed to aid in going beyond the thinker, it is ironic that the thinker is the one who is going to get that state beyond itself."

The word "meditate" in the American College Dictionary means "to engage in thought or contemplation; reflect." The key word here seems to be "reflect." Looking up reflect I found, "1. To mirror; 2. to think carefully." It does not say sitting in some particular position and repeating some mantra or holy words, nor does it say using some device to break the thinking mind to get at a higher self.

There are important questions that come up for me when I examine all this we call meditation (called Mukuso in Japanese Karate): questions help me contemplate, reflect. Questions such as, "Why do we meditate?" and "For what end do we meditate?" and one that is yet deeper, "Who is it that is meditating?" The problem as I see it is not meditation, i.e., the realization that thinking causes a small space around itself blocking out the vastness of living. This is only the first step. The problem comes when the clever mind wants to go beyond itself. It becomes greedy and says, "I want that!" which is just another trick for the ego to sustain itself, to remain in the position of authority, in control. When thinking does this, it creates a division, a split as the thinker (the controller) and thoughts, that which it needs to control. This process is the very reenactment of the original problem. Obviously this is a contradiction, one that many unfortunately fall into.

What meditation means, it seems to me, is to reflect, to mirror what is, to contemplate, to look deeply at what is occurring inside and out. If thinking can observe itself, not doing anything (as the thinker) but just watching, we can begin to see the structure and nature of thought as the thinker, we begin to see how it is put together, how it sustains itself. This awareness, this observation, I would call intelligence, which is also sensitivity, insight. This intelligence sees what prevents understanding and in the process

110

frees itself naturally without the imposition of the thinker. This is a moment to moment movement.

If we have been listening with care to what is being said, we either understand it or have rejected it as nonsense. But if we really see that what we call meditation is vitally important to our practice, in the Art of Karate, in life, then we have grasped the essence of our practice, the process of emptying the self. If we were listening carefully, were intelligently following what was said, were looking at our own minds as we were investigating together, then we were meditating, we were being sensitive, intelligent.

There are two psychological principles in Karate-do which are "mind like water" and "mind like moon." A mind that is still and deep can reflect just what is there; it is an intelligent mind. A mind that has a wide and equal vision, like the moon shining on everything, is a mind that is clear, uncluttered, orderly, free. This mind is the mind of the Karate-ka (the student of Karate) when he or she is practicing with total intensity, with complete spirit. It is a mind that has come about through right understanding, a mind that has no fetters, no limits. What a wonderful thing, this mind!

"By its very nature, the Art of Karate allows the student to lay the right foundation for understanding."

Northern California is so lovely in the Fall and early Winter. The hills are just beginning to turn green from the rains and the yellow mustard is growing wild among the apple trees. How beautiful and wide is the blue sky! An occasional red-winged blackbird glides down to sit on a fencepost or branch. I have seen hawks in the fields. When the mind is quiet, empty, there is living going on in all its magnificence. Thought cannot enter that. Can you see how important it is to be still, quiet, to listen with caring?

Have you ever noticed how Karate belts are tied, and where they hang? They are tied in a square knot and hang just below the navel, in that area called the Hara. The hara is supposedly the seat of the breath, of strength and power. We breathe from there; one's kiai is extended from that area in a sharp verbal retort. The knot that is tied in the belt rests against the hara. There is nothing magical in this. It just reminds me that being essentially a square knot it has the ability to loosen easily when pushed open. But it also has the ability to tighten against itself when pulled on. The harder I pull, the tighter the knot gets. In essence I work against myself when I try to get it untied in this way.

I am reminded of another metaphor— that which is called the Chinese finger puzzle, a wicker tube that I put a finger from each hand into. The object is to get my fingers free. The logical way seems to be by pulling, by retracing the way I got into it. But this only creates more tension and I am all the more captive. If I pull too hard, it will break. The secret of getting free is actually very simple. I have to let go, relax, and keep pushing lightly while holding onto the ends with my other fingers. And out I come!

I am saying all this because it has to do with being able to experience silence— that quality of being which comes about only when one is relaxed, not trying. The knot of our belts and the finger puzzle both remind me of how our minds, how thought, tries to get that which is not of thought, tries to capture and hold the beauty and wonder of livingness in its grasp. It is only when the mind is still, not trying to get anything, when it is just respectfully being aware, that the quality of the living moment has a chance to enter. In Karate practice, when we are training for kata or free style, the mind is in a state of alertness, of silent awareness, allowing that still moment to reflect what is there. In this stillness there is the appropriate response to an immediate challenge.

So these things, like the belt knot by our hara, and a child's toy as simple as the Chinese finger puzzle, can be reminders for us, to show us how we work, how we prevent ourselves from being able to go beyond the isolated self to something far greater, vaster, more awesome. Karate is not merely punching and kicking. That is only self-defense. The Art of Karate is far more meaningful than that. When we practice, we can become aware of all the little reminders that point toward something deeper, like sign posts along an endless, unknown journey.

"It is only through the practice of form and understanding what the Art of Karate is all about that you can really benefit from your time here."

Perhaps I speak more to the young people than the adults about the issue of advancement, of rank, of the belts that go along with accomplishment, as an outward symbol of that feat. I think the Black Belt has a great deal of symbolic power now in our culture. It represents to many the ability to do strange and wondrous things, to defend oneself from many foes, like in the Westerns where the good guy always wins. I think that has been conditioned into younger people. As adults we become quite clever in our worship of success, quite cunning in getting what we set out for. Power shows itself in business or in conquering a mate (what we call romance). I know that many adults desire to have this symbol of achievement, as perhaps another feather in their cap, another notch in their gun, another confirmation of the ego.

How many of you are envisioning the Black Belt? Look at this piece of material around my waist. What do you see when you look at it? Color, shape, form, texture? There is a striking contrast of the Black Belt on the white gi. Very stark, outstanding.

What else do you see? Power, accomplishment, experience? Yes? But is that in the belt or in your mind? If it is in your mind, where did it come from? I wonder how many of you would be here if we had no belts? Now, who wants to be a volunteer? Come on up here. Okay, Chris, you be the volunteer. Here, try this Black Belt on. Shall we do our basics now?

(Thirty minutes later)

Let's sit down and talk some more. Chris, what did you feel wearing the belt? You felt embarrassed and yet powerful...why? You felt embarrassed because you had not earned the belt. And you felt powerful because you were still wearing it. Yes, I understand that.

Can you see that you give some symbolic significance, some power to this piece of material? The belt should stand for something or why wear it? It does not hold up my pants, it serves no utilitarian purpose. It serves as an award of accomplishment, a symbol of experience and respect for that accomplishment. But I think we see much more in it than this. If we are looking at the belts as tokens of power, as a reward, then we are defeating our purpose here. To look at them as such fabricates an external or outside motivation. Do you know what I mean? You lose the love of doing Karate for itself and start to do it for the reward, the payment, whether it be a Black Belt, money, status, degrees or whatever. This kind of power-seeking only creates more ego, more inflation, more filling up...not emptying out.

When you are here practicing, be aware of why you are here, what you want. Don't judge it, just watch it and you will learn something about yourself. It is natural to want to have the Black Belt but be careful how you go about it. Looking toward that belt removes you from your practice, your form. Practice your form and belts will come of them-selves, not as a reward but as a genuinely deserved award.

The young mind is so open, so simple, and then there are the demands of this violent life.

How can we prepare the young mind to meet life intelligently, so it can remain sensitive and innocent?

"People who are denying aggression for the ideal of nonaggression, or nonviolence, are paradoxically, by the very act of denial, doing violence to themselves as a result."

When we really love to do something we find we have a good deal of energy to do it. Conversely, when we don't want to do something we have very little energy for it, but there is also sometimes a lot of energy wasted in resisting what we don't want to do.

Energy is the life force. Energy is the creative reservoir that helps us to do what we want to do. It is the force behind all great enterprise, it is the inspiration needed to develop a strong practice in the dojo. Energy is the vitality we feel after we have worked hard and done well, and we recognize it as such. Energy is power and strength. Mainly, energy comes from the mind; when the mind sees clearly, there is complete, immediate, unimpeded action. The mind, through breath, moves the body into action.

Living with a great deal of energy is what I would call living with passion. Obviously I don't mean sexual love or violent anger; what I mean is a strong enthusiasm for the art, a zest for living. The more passion we contain, the more we come alive.

In the Art of Karate we talk a great deal about aggression, or violating another, assaulting or attacking someone. This violation or assault can be either physical or verbal, gross or subtle. We talk about aggression because we want to understand it, go beyond it. The Art of Karate is a vehicle that aids us in understanding aggression, not creating more aggression to battle the existing aggression, not an "eye for an eye," as is practiced globally today. We engage aggression, delve into it, even as we would with a problem of health; we look at the symptoms and go to the cause. This is not always the case with people. Today there is a rejection of aggression, a denial of anything that hints at aggressiveness. The overenthusiasm for aggression is simply the counterphobia, the denial of the denial. Many people, on hearing that I teach Karate, back off because they are afraid of this, or they embrace it disingenuously. The "New Age" movement is one that seems to deny aggression, which sets up a conflict between the fact of what is and the ideal of what should be.

Let's take it from another perspective. If we have grown up in a society that is aggressive, that has become competitive and violent because it lives by ideals, then we are a part of that society, we are the aggression; it is us! There comes a point in our lives when we want to be rid of this aggression, in ourselves and in the world. This is a worthy and necessary endeavor, to want to live peacefully, in harmony with ourselves and others. What happens in this logic is that we think the way to be rid of aggression is to deny it, to eradicate it. What we don't see is that we are the violence, the aggression.

What usually happens— and I call this the "Paradox of Change"— is that in order to convert from a state of aggression to nonaggression, a person first labels the aggression as bad, evil, then creates the ideal, the logical opposite of aggression and violence— the good or Godlike. One usually, but not always, finds some personification for the goodness; a hero, a religious person, for example.

Now the person approximates his or her actions to an image of goodness, in other words, they affect behavior, become proper or religious. The task is at hand, according to this logical process of constantly striving to be good or Godlike. Nothing less than perfection, the highest good, is desired.

What these people have failed to see is that, in their desire to eliminate or deny aggression and violence, they have created a division, a split between what is (aggression) and what should be (nonaggression). This division, this split, is a state of conflict, a state of violence. In order to achieve goodness by their method, they must deny what is, and eradicate it. They forget the simple fact...they *are* the aggression, the aggression is them. The harder they try to become good the more they have to eliminate the bad, i.e. themselves.

Their minds have set up a duality, a struggle inside the mind between the me who is the ideal, goodness, and the not-me, who translates as badness. The more we try to be good, the more we experience the bad because they are one and the same movement, the same process of thought. We are tricked into thinking that the badness is not in us, and that it can therefore be eradicated by this method. When it does not work (it can't because of the very self-destructive, self-contradictory nature of it), we begin to seek external support or weight for the side of goodness. The mind creates a "religion."

This struggle is manifested outwardly in competition, with oneself and others; eventually the inner war becomes the outer war. Instead of understanding that the judgment as "bad" is self-created, we project it onto others. It is then "they" who are bad, who oppose, not us. We have identified with the image of goodness and have disowned the image of being bad onto others. "It is the Russians who are evil," we say. But that is what the Russians say about us.

Only when we begin to see the nature of the problem, how it is creating conflict through ideals, do we have a chance to change. Becoming aware of the problem is the beginning of understanding; it is the first step to its resolution. When we do not set up this pendulum of good and bad, the me controlling myself, then there is freedom from that conflict. This begins harmonious movement, which grows. When we deny aggression, we deny the real passion, the real energy needed to understand the problem. The harder we try to be good, the less passion we have, because conformity to the ideal is a state of rigidity.

"Violence is the process of perpetuating the self, and this perpetuating of me is the root and cause of the competition we call business."

The other day I went into the local bookstore as I sometimes do to browse around. I came across a book that I had seen before, a book that has been recommended as an important text for all serious Martial Arts students. It is A Book of Five Rings by Miyamoto Musashi.

I looked through the pages and read selections. I was confused. I read about a man, who decided he was going to play Samurai to prove himself and went out and became a swordsman. He killed his first person at the age of thirteen! He continued killing people for many years, and was defeated only once in all his endeavors (apparently with no injury to himself). He then retired to a retreat and towards the end of his life he wrote this book.

His account is about strategy, how to deal successfully with an opponent. I won't go into all the clever details here with you today. What I do want to share with you is how people have seen and are using the Martial Arts in destructive, unethical ways. Musashi was, in blunt terms, a murderer. That he should glorify or justify his actions in spiritual-sounding language through this book astounds me! I feel this man is not understanding the Martial Arts at all, but is making a tremendous perversion of what is in essence a nonviolent and gentle discipline. Some people have said to me that it was indicative of his era and that he did what he had to do. But was there ever a time in the history of humanity when killing another human being could be justified?

I was shocked even further by what I read on the cover: "A National Best Seller!", "Japan's Answer to the Harvard MBA!", "On Wall Street, When Musashi Talks, People Listen," all quotes from Time magazine. Inside the jacket cover the boasts continue: "The book corporate America is taking into the Boardrooms!" and "A strategy for gentleman warriors" from the <u>New York Times</u>. On the inside cover there was also a small biographical account of Miyamoto Musashi, that I would like to read to you. I think it is appropriate. It says, "Born in 1584, Miyamoto Musashi was destined to become one of Japan's most renowned warriors. He was a Samurai and, by the age of thirty, had fought and won more than sixty contests by killing all of his opponents. Satisfied that he was invincible, Musashi then turned to formulating his philosophy of 'the way of the sword.' He wrote <u>A Book of Five Rings</u> (Gorin No Sho) while living in a cave in the mountains of Kyosho a few weeks before his death in 1645.

"<u>A Book of Five Rings</u> heads every Martial Arts bibliography; but the philosophy behind it — influenced by Zen, Shinto and Confucianism — can be applied to many areas of life other than the Martial Arts. For example, many entrepreneurial Japanese businessmen use it today as a guide for business practice, running sales campaigns like military operations with the same energy that motivated Musashi."

Much of this is perhaps motivated by an over-zealousness to get the book sold (a "military operation" in itself), but what is sadly true is that many people, especially in business, do consciously or unconsciously feel like this, or feel that they have to, that business is a battle, run like a war. With competition getting greater, as is its nature, there is much more emphasis on winning.

This whole movement of wanting to become like a Samurai is a terribly destructive, romantic notion. It is just another way to glorify the self. Musashi wanting to become invincible, it seems to me, is just another example (although quite an extreme one) of his deep-rooted fear of death and the dying of the psychological self so that one is nothing, is a nobody.

There is an old saying that, "The wrong man with the right tools comes out with the wrong results." This is particularly true when a person tries to use the Martial Arts as a path to self-importance, self-aggrandizement. This self-importance and self-inflation are the opposite of the intention of the Art of Karate. In Karate we are beginning to understand the causes of violence and this is the essence of our practice in Take Nami Do. It is a war — inside of us — a constant struggle between self as the thinker, and thoughts. This internal battle is externalized as competition, the struggle not only with oneself but also with all other selves. It is our intention in Karate to understand this terribly violent process. This is the main reason why we practice. If we don't, then our practice becomes destructive also, in that it will only feed the need to be someone, somebody, to prove ourselves, which is another form of competition. Practice, if done right, wears the false idealism out of us. Can we now begin to really see our purpose with the Art of Karate, that is, to empty the self, to live as nobody, as nothing?

In the words of Leonardo DaVinci: *"Among the greatest things to be found among us, the Being of Nothingness is by far the greatest."*

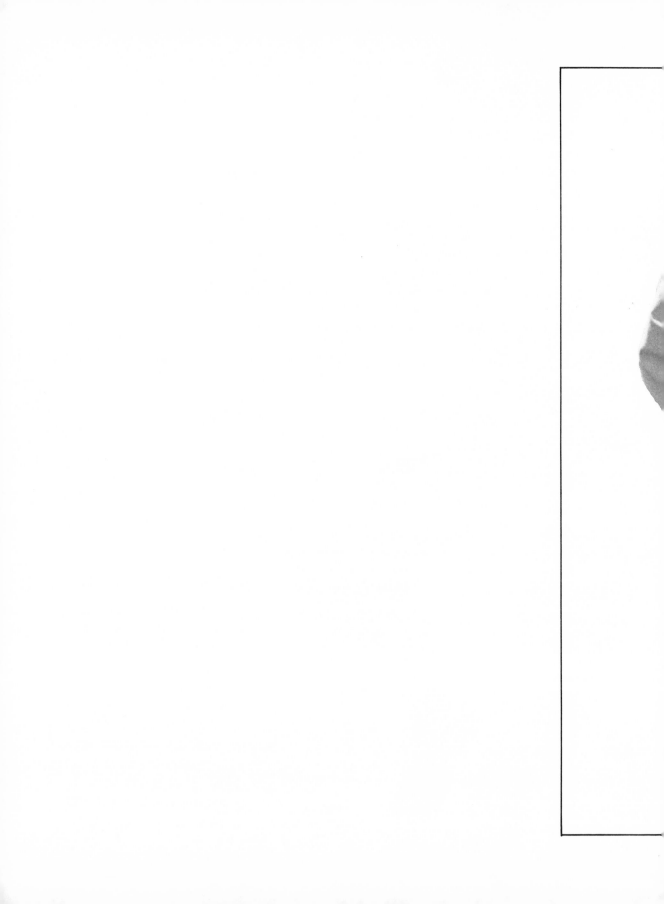

Poised in a stance of combat the body is ready to meet the challenge of attack. At this moment there is a psychological pause—a suspension of the momentum of the past, the demands of the self. Time has ended and with it the reaction to protect and defend. There is only the gesture and limitless space with no center as the "me."

"One loses the love of the thing itself, and does it not for that but for the prize of adulation, of approval, glorification."

Why is it that man needs to prove himself, in competition, by pitting one against another to see who is the victor? It seems to me to be such a childish thing. This competition destroys all sensitivity; it is a goal-oriented, externally motivated reward that takes a person away from being aware of the act itself. This process denies one the ability to look deeper; it keeps a person at a superficial level.

I started formally practicing the Art of Karate in 1961. Back in the 60s I went to quite a few tournaments, mostly in New York City where I was living (I also competed in a tournament given by Chuck Norris in California in the mid-60s). I felt these tournaments were just ways to prove oneself. They had little, as I could see, to do with the real Art form. There were kata competitions, but even they were another way to prove who was the best.

Why do we need to do this? Why are we using Karate, and other Martial Arts, as vehicles to show who is the greatest, most accomplished? It seems to me that this attitude is at the animal level in us, a need to display prowess, fighting skills, as males of various species do, mainly during the mating season.

At these Martial Arts tournaments contestants tended to become more and more aggressive and violent, especially in free style. There were, in those days, many accidents, when the lack of control caused injury. It was all a part of the macho image of being tough, taking punishment. It was like rutting animals. This was certainly not the Karate I was seeking. I had intuited something more spiritual in the Martial Arts than this, something far more intelligent and nonviolent.

There were those who proved themselves with feats of breaking bricks, splitting boards, ice, and almost anything they could get their hands and feet on. Others enacted daring feats with sharp swords, like cutting an apple placed on the neck of a person while blindfolded. I remember one fellow who crashed his head into roofing tiles and another who used his head to break a 300-pound block of ice! The audience seemed to love these bizarre displays of power. But all along I felt that there was something wrong with all of this. I think what finally did it for me was pictures I saw of a Karate teacher killing a bull. Then I personally witnessed a Kung Fu teacher skin a live snake with his teeth!

Years later I read Gichin Funakoski's book, My Way of Life and at last began to understand that this Martial Art I was studying could be something far different from what I had seen in those tournaments, something I had felt but had little external support for. I had finally begun to understand the Art of Karate. I knew inside that Karate was not to be studied just to become tougher and more macho. The world was violent enough. I felt that such an art form could bring about a real sense of gentleness and understanding. What I was learning about the body, with its ability to store fear and aggression, was now another insight into how the Art of Karate could aid in the healthful needs of the serious student. Karate could allow deep psychophysical work in the body, freeing a person from pent-up tension and disease.

Today, many years after my experience with the early tournaments, I still find the violence of proving oneself, not only in the Martial Arts but in most everything we do. Full contact Karate is quite popular. It is getting more and more professional. I fear that the real spirit of the Art could be lost in all this professionalism. A student starts out with idealistic notions of Karate, which may include some vague understanding of spirituality and mysticism. Because they start out with ideals, which are just projections of self, they only seem to create more reinforcement for self via competition, in proving oneself.

There are the exceptions to the rule in tournaments. If one has the right attitude and wants to understanding him- or herself and can find this opportunity in a well-designed tournament, run with sensitivity and intelligence, then that student can only benefit from that experience. But unfortunately this is the exception. I personally know of only one annual tournament that seems intelligent. Perhaps there are more, but my experience lately is limited in this area.

If a serious student does start out with the right attitude and understanding, it is becoming increasingly hard to find support for wanting Karate to be something really meaningful, significant, something that will be beneficial to mankind.

"One can, sensing a potential attack, being non-defensive, open, alert, turn that potential for destruction into something constructive."

Yesterday I was outside watching the neighbor's cat. She was lying in the sun, seemingly asleep. A flying insect of some sort came buzzing by her. With a very surprising darting motion the cat had moved in a flash from her resting position to bat that flying bug. It was astonishing how incredibly quick she was. She moved from a relaxed, sleep-like position to a state of complete alertness within a fraction of a second! And there was no tension in her movements.

What surprised me most about the cat was that she had no formal training in what she did. She was not a highly skilled Karate master, having been dedicated to years of diligent and disciplined practice. Naturally and spontaneously she moved from a resting position to attack that insect. It seemed as if she was just playing.

As we have mentioned many times, the Art of Karate is a great deal more than a mere set of physical self-defense skills. If one were taking Karate for only this or just to prove oneself, puff up one's ego, then we would not have the Art, the essence of Karate-do. There is the reality of learning a self-defense, but there is also the paradox of learning a self-defense so one has no need to defend the self. In order to have no need to be defensive, to prove and protect the self, one must work very hard in Karate basics: the blocking, punching, kicking and striking that is essentially the core of the physical self-defense system. One must work very hard to gain the real confidence that one needs psychologically in order to be free from the deep-rooted fears, and the resulting defensiveness, anger, tension, stress, and aggression in competition.

We must practice for a long time to be skillful, to be confident in our basics, fix style, and free style. It takes quite a while to be able to move quickly, spontaneously, to

129

neutralize an attack in free style even before the other has time to carry out his or her attack on you. This quality of sensing the attack and responding before it can be brought against you takes a quality of mind and body that is highly sensitive, highly skillful.

There is another seemingly contradictory aspect to all this. Although we must train diligently for many years to be as swift as the cat, as skillful and spontaneous as the cat's ability to attack, we must also be able to be spontaneous right from the beginning of our practice. Although our naturalness comes from years of training, it also comes from our ability to "play," to allow ourselves to be "playful." I think the key here, as with the cat, is being attentive, aware, in our yoi or ready stance. The cat is naturally alert, attentive, without formal training. It is her innate survival instinct. We also have this ability, partially learned and partially intuitive.

If we practice only in the formal training, only in repetition of technique, then we will become one-sided; we will become mechanical, stiff, inflexible. We must also allow for that natural sense of responding to occur, to allow for one's sense of spontaneity. This is what I call playing. Therefore the combination of learned skills and natural, innate, survival reactions, create a person who is well-rounded, one who is capable of responding, in the case of Karate, to the attack before it happens.

"Without this deeper understanding, the inquiry into the mind, then Karate is merely a set of gymnastic skills."

Today there is a great abundance of sports; you can see them on television. Not only the major American sports of baseball, football, and basketball, but World Cup soccer and all the varied and many sports that we see in the Olympics. Millions of people spend many millions of dollars to watch sports. Also many play a sport on a regular basis.

I'm not against sports. They can be fun and definitely have a place in life. What I find a problem is the over-emphasis of sports, the amount of money that professional athletes get for their endeavors. I find this a disconcerting issue in our society, a society that is already saturated with entertainment of all sorts.

Much of sports, as I said, seems a good and healthy activity. Sports are also a way to prove oneself, to show one's physical prowess. There are many people who want Karate to be a sport, to have big-time competition, to show who is the best, who is the top Karate-ka.

Karate, to me, is much more than a sport. If Karate were only a physical discipline it could not do what it does; that is, serve as a vehicle to aid the student in understanding him- or herself, in bringing about an internal transformation. If Karate were only a physical discipline it would soon die out; the students would probably stop practicing, unless there were continuous competitions as an outlet for the sports-minded individuals among them. If you are practicing Karate merely as a set of physical movements you will end up with very little. A dancer can move, can even imitate Karate moves. But a dancer does not practice the Art of Karate. Nor does an athlete.

The Art of Karate as a physical discipline is still important. It is the manifestation of some of the deeper aspects of its psychological function. The Art of Karate is mainly mental, psychological, in that one must have a deep under-

131

standing of the essence of Karate, in order to empty oneself.

As you practice, see what you do, watch your practice, observe how much time is spent on the physical, how much on the mental. Do you (since you have only a limited time at the dojo) spend time outside examining Karate principles and integrating them into your life? If your commitment is merely going to practice two times a week and working out, then you are not doing Karate; you would be better off staying home and watching television or playing baseball. But if you see the importance of the psychology of Karate as well, then your very life becomes a vehicle for understanding. Then you will be living the Art as your life.

"If we judge, we just set up more resistance and we cannot see what the problem is, where it comes from, how it comes into being."

There is a wise old saying, "In Karate they say: if practicing basics is boring, after two minutes, try it for four. If it is still boring, try it for eight, sixteen, thirty-two, and so on. Eventually one discovers that it's not boring at all but very interesting."

I think that it is hard to go to practice sometimes when we would rather be somewhere else, watching television, or whatever. Practice is hard work. We have built up resistance to it, even before we get to practice, we have set ourselves up for boredom and the pain of resistance. Therefore when we arrive we are unconsciously, or perhaps even consciously, defensive. If this is happening we do not allow the present moment to speak to us. We are closed off, resisting the moment. This is actually conflict, this division of mentally wanting to be somewhere else, fighting the moment. It is a problem we seem to create a lot for ourselves, not only here in the dojo, but at our jobs, in school, and at home. This resistance to what is, this wanting something else, this disliking what is going on now, is a form of comparison — comparing one moment to a previously experienced one, feeling that there is something wrong with this moment. This comes from our need to be distracted, to be entertained; because most likely our lives are troublesome, stress-producing. Perhaps our jobs are not fulfilling, school is a punishing experience, our relationships are filled with problems. This way of dealing with our problems by distraction, by entertainment, leads only to worse problems.

It seems that if Karate can really mean something to us, help us live our lives more healthfully, sanely, then it is important to look at our lives, to see the resistance and boredom at the dojo. It is important to begin there and work outward, so to speak, because the Art of Karate really is a way of life, our whole life.

Can we begin to observe this boredom and resistance in class? In order to do this we must watch nonjudgmentally. We must be empty and present.

"In our practice it is important to listen, to take that quality of attention with us away from our dojo, with us throughout our day."

Let's try a little experiment. Close your eyes and just listen. Can you listen to all the sounds equally...just sounds, rising and falling, one replacing another. Can you just listen to the chatter in your head, that voice you call "I" or "me," just listen to it as just another noise? How many different sounds are you aware of? Are you labeling what you hear? Are you saying, "Oh, that's a squirrel chattering," or "a plane in the distance," or "the neighbor's dog barking," or "myself talking inside myself?" Can you just listen without recognition of what it is you hear? Can you also just watch the mind, its thoughts, coming up like bubbles from the void, rising and then going away? Or are you caught by them, unaware of the rest of the sounds around you, thinking of what happened yesterday, thinking of your vacation next week, or whatever you are thinking?

I wonder if we see the value in just listening. We are so used to gaining, from exploiting, from getting some profit, product, or result from what we do, that I wonder if we can really see the significance of just listening. Listening reads between the lines, so to speak. It is an alert quality of attention that is also deeply sensitive.

I wonder if we really ever listen. We hear a lot: television, movies, our teachers, parents, friends speaking constantly. Perhaps we are overloaded and need to turn it all off. Can we listen to what is being said? It is only through really listening that we can hear the truth or falseness of something. If we listen with care we will be able to find out what is below the surface, what is ordinarily hidden when we only hear.

Yesterday morning I was awakened by the neighbor. He was working on his house. Banging nails and an electric saw were crashing in on my sleep. Before I was fully awake I found myself just listening to them; although they were

In the proper deliverance of form, the body's wisdom comes forth. One's innate power manifests itself and there is great strength. One may be old in years, but if one's spirit is allowed to blossom because one has developed a structure and form for it, the youthfulness of creative energy is touched and displayed in one's actions, not only in the Art of Karate but in all aspects of everyday living.

loud, they were not a nuisance. Then I observed my critical mind arising: "It's Sunday morning and he shouldn't be working, making that noise! Can't he see that this is not proper relationship when he is making so much noise?" I felt that he should be more sensitive, more aware of his neighbors around him, rather than only being concerned for his needs. There are times when a person can work and not disturb his neighbors. But my rightness didn't help the fact of the noise right at that moment; in fact, it made it intolerable! I was resisting it because I thought I was right and he was wrong. Granted, I could have gone over to his place and asked him to stop, but instead I just began to listen again to the noise, and other noises. The distraction of the saw was softened by just listening, became more a part of a whole symphony of sounds called life. The less I judged, the less I resisted, the more I could just listen. It helped put things back in perspective.

The Art of Karate is a way of life, not something you just do in the dojo.

"We become the form, we are the form and the form is an expression of life within and without, it is life moving through us."

I have talked a great deal about the essence of Karate-do, about "emptying oneself." It seems that all Karate practice is the essence of this emptying. It is a very simple yet paradoxically complex process. I feel it is worth our time to look at it from every angle to see what it is we are doing in Karate. If it is just self defense we are looking for, I suggest we arm ourselves or buy a guard dog. If we are just looking for a physical exercise or a sport, perhaps baseball, swimming, jogging or tennis would be better. But if we seek internal change and harmony rather than a self-defense, a physical exercise or sport, then we are candidates for the discipline of Karate.

I have noticed that many students practice to become more powerful, develop technique that is strong, invincible. Many students are also looking towards advancement in rank as an outward recognition of that power. I have noticed that when we are striving to attain power and recognition, we are so tight and tense, so bent on attaining our goal, that our muscles are used against us. We don't allow for the flexibility needed for real power. We are constricting our body, pushing ourselves to be strong—and we forget our form.

I have walked behind men in practice as they are tensing and have put my hands on their shoulders, holding them back and down so they don't tense up, so they don't reach too far forward in their movements. Women are more naturally suited for Karate it seems, because they have not been conditioned like men to be "manly" and strong. Men are habituated to accomplish by sheer will power, through the muscular effort of exertion. This is not good for our practice. Our need to achieve, to become stronger, more powerful by using effort and will power must be abandoned.

Real power comes from form. When we can practice form

correctly, speed comes naturally, and out of speed, combined with the technique of form comes power, of its own! There is nothing will power can do to get this power except to practice form. It is form first and always. Form is practicing movements correctly, with patience, with great attention to each delicate and precise momentary movement. It is a moment-to-moment process creating a level of awareness that sees the subtle, minute qualities of each movement. A natural, graceful ease is generated in practicing form. This effortless practicing of form can also lay the foundation for something greater — but we must not rely on this, we must not make this a new goal.

"There is only intelligent perception and in that there is immediate action."

At night I sometimes hear the wind chimes outside my cottage door, the gentle night wind blowing through and around the brass cylinders causing them to clang into each other. Then the hooting of a nearby owl. I sometimes walk out and look up at the night sky. The tiny white flickering stars, the great expanse of space; the mind boggles at the view, the perception of seeming endlessness. A thought bubbles up, "Am I looking out into endless space, or down into endless space, or sideways?" A slight feeling of disorientation, falling, then the thought passes as quickly as it came, back into the void. The tall trees in the dark night loom overhead, reaching out to the stars, to the sun from which all things came. The wonder of night ceases all questioning. The mind's usual activity is quieted in the awesomeness of the night.

Questions that some people ask on first coming into the dojo are, "How long does it take to get a Black Belt?" and "Do you do full contact?" I find that these people rarely come back after we talk. Their questions aren't really serious. Strangely I get very few questions about what I teach in Karate. I actually worry when some parents leave their children with me and don't ask what I do.

This question of full contact comes up often and I want to address it briefly. There is a movement in the Martial Arts, especially in Karate, that wants to have full-contact competition matches. It is very popular. Again, I see this desire for full-contact as a need to test one's power, to compete to prove how strong one is. I find it rather sad that one would have to prove how strong they are.

In the United States boxing is a very popular activity. If I remember correctly, in the last championship fights the winners split fourteen million dollars! The man who won said he would consider a rematch with the man he beat but only for twenty-one million dollars for himself! When I think of the dedicated teachers who live on so little I shudder at what is happening.

I can understand when a person asks if we have full contact fighting. Perhaps their hopes are to become professionals and make money. Professional Karate is on the rise. With incentives of millions of dollars in boxing I can see why people would want to learn full contact. This may not be the only reason. There is also the need to test one's prowess. Personally I feel no need to demonstrate my Karate skill. It is not for display, to exhibit for others to see. It is a personal thing, that I share with myself as the moment moves me.

Although we do make light contact in blocking, which is necessary to get the feel of it, we do not make contact as an attack or counter-attack. There are times when we misjudge and contact but this is to be expected. In order to really develop full power, we cannot make contact. A thin piece of styrofoam cannot protect a person from a full power technique. We practice with full power because it allows us the discipline of pulling our attacks, of stopping just short of our target. Therefore our form is at its best. We are not indulging in mere street fighting, hitting each other just to see who is stronger.

A full point in our style means that you have successfully completed correct form, you have stopped and controlled your attack. It allows for the setting of limits within the form practiced. This also is important to us psychologically in that it demonstrates our ability to be able to set safe limits on our behavior. It aids us in feeling the real confidence in full power that we need psychologically to be confident enough not to fight in a real situation...confident enough to use more creative, nonviolent ways of solving conflict.

Can we really see the truth of this, or is it all just words, someone who is telling us what to do? I am not telling anyone what to do. I am only sharing observations. Perhaps another will also see what we do. Then what I have said is not mine. It is what is, the truth. In understanding, in seeing what is true, we are moving together; there is no

disagreement, my opinion against yours. There is no conflict when we both see the truth.

*Can the Art of Karate bring
to our attention the need to
understand and go beyond
conflict...*

or is it just another
manifestation of
mankind's compulsion
for violence?

ENLIGHTENMENT

"To enlighten means 'to shed light upon.' It makes sense therefore that enlightenment is understanding who we are, staying with the fact, the truth of what is and not indulging in the projections of self-centered, wishful thinking."

The word "enlightenment" has been used lately in reference to the Martial Arts and the practice of Zen, called Zazen or sitting meditation. What is enlightenment? What does it mean to be enlightened? It seems that the clever mind, the ego, the "me" has formulated a belief and projected that belief as an ideal, a belief that there is a peaceful state beyond our suffering. This is what we hope for and yet our hopes only add more suffering. What we don't see is that suffering comes from hope. These are one and the same process. What we don't see is that suffering comes from not facing the fact; it comes from creating the illusion of what should be, which is enlightenment, an idyllic place where one is free from the pain of self-centered action. We don't see that creating the ideal of enlightenment is just more self-centered action. Or perhaps we do see all this but are too stubborn and self-centered, so we just keep trying to be enlightened.

Isn't this enlightenment just our vanity? Isn't it our own little egos wanting to continue forever? We read of enlightenment in books, or some "enlightened person" tells us about it and we believe in it, we desire it. Isn't this only a form of greed, the greed of self-centered activity? We may see that the problems of relationship are the isolation and fragmentation of each ego caught in its own world of make believe. We may have this insight but what happens then? The ego identifies with another hope, as enlightenment, and sustains its fragmentary and isolated activity, continuing to bring more conflict to the world. When will we see the danger and violence of this? We talk endlessly about reform, the social, economic, political, educational or religious reforms, but our problems continue. What we don't see fundamentally is that the problem is us, not something imposed on or happening to us.

So we ask, what can we do? The ego just seems to continue no matter what we do to get rid of it! What we don't see is that the "I" who wants to get rid of the ego and the ego are one and the same. There is no divided self capable of ending itself. This is the fundamental illusion, the fundamental source of conflict. But if there is nothing we can do to end the isolated and self-centered activity of the ego, what then? Just live with it?

We read so many books, we try so many activities, we have become so overly educated in the psychological realm. The New Age movement in Psychology is primarily based on ways to end this basic problem. The mind has invented endless paths to salvation or enlightenment. And the problems get worse. Can't we see that the very act of salvation, of wanting to be enlightened, is the cause of the violence we are trying to end?

It is really such a simple thing, to see this paradoxical situation. In the Martial Arts, Zen and Zazen are seen as important parts of this training. People who practice Zazen say that they are only sitting, just to be aware; or that they are aware while walking or in going through the activity of their daily lives. They say that one should sit without thinking, to be empty, like a mirror, with no attachments. They say that Zazen is not a means to enlightenment; they say Zazen is enlightenment. But isn't this just another clever trick of the ego? Zazen comes from thought itself, it is the product of thought. Zazen's commandment is to be like a mirror, just be aware without thinking. But we are constantly thinking. This is the fact. Not thinking is the ideal, the "should be," the desire to be what we are not, which again is just more of the same conflict. To say Zazen is enlightenment is to say that a mountain is a river; both are illusions.

All one can do is to be what one is. There is no division of ideals and hence no conflict. When we are what we are, what occurs? Either we justify who we are and lose ourselves in the self-centered expression of that, in indulgence, or we begin to become aware of what makes us do what we do. Being aware is not a trick of the ego. It is simply being aware, which has nothing to do with any practice, any method or path, or way. It is simply awareness. Awareness cannot be attained...awareness is not the outcome of thought. Awareness is intelligence. When there is intelligence, there is understanding. It is understanding that brings light to our problem, which is us. We cannot practice awareness, intelligence. Practicing to be aware, to be intelligent, is unintelligent. It will only dull the mind.

Awareness is a mirror of the fact. The fact is that the mind is caught in a maze of convoluted, self-indulgent thinking. The fact is that this confused state of mind thinks it can solve the problem it has created by the very same process that created the problem in the first place. To say that we must sit Zazen without thinking is wishful thinking. It is just more control, more fear, more self-centered activity and hence more conflict. We cannot command the mind to stop thinking, for isn't the "commander" the "commanded," the thinker the thoughts? Can we really see the truth of this? Or is this just more assertive opinion, or dogmatic belief? How will we find out if this is true?

Isn't enlightenment really just being simply aware, aware of what is actually going on? There are so many people who can talk and write so convincingly, but when their actual day-to-day lives are observed, there is little awareness. We can so easily learn educated-sounding words and create the illusion of understanding.

Can we just be aware, aware of the so-called ordinary occurrence of daily life? Can we be aware of how we eat, how we stand or sit, aware of how we drop our clothes on the floor, or leave our dirty dishes for others to clean? Can we be aware of the moment, each and every moment, which includes not only the many self-indulgent habits we have, but also to see the constant chattering of the fearful, ego-centered mind, all the images it makes, the identification with these images, the dream world we live in? Can we be aware, without any motive or commandment, of the totality of each moment? Then the mind is intelligent, then it is like a mirror, because it reflects the fact, the truth, the endless desires. Perhaps we don't see clearly because we talk too much, because we see through our minds, through thought and all the manifestations of thought. This is where we can start, just to see the confusion and to stay with the fact of that.

*How does that quality of attention come about,
that is needed to burn through
confused and timid self-protective thinking?
Can we see the danger of it
and so seeing, wake up?*

PART IV
OBSERVATIONS

The intention of this section is to stimulate inquiry into the activities of human behavior, as it is manifested in the context of the Art of Karate, and as it is already manifest in our daily lives, for the Art of Karate and life are not separate; they are one unified movement. If one is serious about the practice of the Art of Karate then one will naturally want to understand its implications to the rest of living. In order to inquire into human behavior it is important to understand what this process is, that is, how we approach such an issue.

Inquiry is not dogmatic assertions. Inquiry is not any fixed conclusion one has about life, an opinion one wants to force on another. In other words, inquiry is not a psychological manipulation, a form of conditioning thought and behavior.

Inquiry is intelligence, the capacity of insight, the ability to see into the nature of things, to understand life as it is. Inquiry starts from an insight and moves from insight to insight. In inquiry the question always arises, "What is the intelligent thing to do?"

Inquiry is philosophy in its true definition: the love of truth in everyday life. Philosophy has become formulated in ideals, in belief. Truth is understanding; truth is perception. Belief creates the illusion of what we hope life could be. Truth, insight, intelligence is understanding life as it is.

Inquiry is the movement of intelligence. It is not static. Inquiry is observation. It is the ability to see into things as they are. Inquiry does not create the illusion of ideals; it stays with the fact of what is and in so doing, understands it. Thought is used as a means of conveying the insight that observation has revealed. Thought is not the act of observation, of inquiry. It is only the vehicle for transmitting what was seen. Thought removed from observation, from insight, can create a maze of clever intellectual jargon to convince itself of its authority. This jargon creates the ideal of understanding. Understanding is not an ideal; it is learning in the present moment.

The conventional approach to understanding is based on tradition, on conclusions, fixed opinions about life. This convention is based solely on the intellectual capacity; that is, thought generating only more thought. Perhaps at the beginning of the traditional approach there was a fundamental insight, but this soon deteriorated into belief as thought took over.

So to inquire into the nature of human behavior and the Art of Karate, the mind cannot be caught in opinion, in any conditioned conclusion about life. The mind must be alert, sensitive, active. This means it is constantly learning, observing the continuous unfolding process of the dynamic movement of living.

The concept SHUHARI is important to understand in Take Nami Do Karate. SHU means learning from tradition; HA means breaking the chains of tradition; and RI means transcendence. It is necessary to learn the traditional way in Karate. Too often we get fixed there, we come to worship the tradition, to find security in it. We become afraid to move beyond it and in so doing we build a prison around ourselves. We must learn from tradition and at some point let observation bring its own intelligence to bear upon this tradition. As we practice the prescribed way, there will be moments when we are aware of a natural impulse, an organic movement, if I can use that word. This impulse is HA, the act of observation that by its very nature changes that which it observes. There is at this point a merger of the old and the new. This is the creative act and needs to be expressed. This impulse, when it is not self-serving, will enhance one's form, will bring passion to it, will give it spirit, life. Without HA, the form becomes stale, old, dead.

154

When the creative impulse of HA is allowed its natural movement, we have entered RI, transcendence. We go beyond the form as a rote repetition of technique and go into the form as something alive. This is the meaning of SHUHARI.

The Art of Karate is more than practicing self-defense techniques. The Art of Karate is reflected in everything we do, for living itself is the highest art form. Understanding this, things find their right order.

Is there a place for ritual in Karate? People have used ritual to evoke the divine, to gain a religious experience. This seems to be the wrong approach. Can ritual be used instead to create a context, a framework to express what is beauty? In Take Nami Do Karate we have Rank Ceremonies to celebrate the accomplishment of students' work. It is a ritual in that we dress up in our more formal Karate attire and we present a program for the parents and friends attending. I personally find ritual used in this way to be a means of creating an affectionate relationship between students and students, students and teachers, and students and their parents, partners and friends.

In Japan the expression "loss of face" means to suffer humiliation, to lose one's honor. Some people regard this very seriously and have even taken their lives after losing face. Hari Kari is the formal practice of taking one's own life. This is such a terribly sad thing. Why would someone want to take their own life if they "lose face?" What does it mean to lose face? What is there to lose? Is it the image we have about ourselves? Is it our reputation, success, achievement, or rank we have achieved in society? We see ourselves through the eyes of others, and in so doing we judge ourselves, compare ourselves to another. This comparison makes us feel either inferior or superior, both of which are born out of fear, the fear of not being, not becoming. Isn't this self pride? Don't we need the respect of others and when we don't get it we feel crushed, humiliated, hurt? What is it that gets hurt? Isn't it our self-image of how great we think we are? When others don't like what we do we feel degraded, disgraced, dishonored, and we cannot look at this because it conflicts with our self-image, our self-image of how noble, illustrious, and proud we feel. The word "prestige" means "having a reputation or influence arising from success, achievement, rank;" or "distinction attaching to a person and dominating the minds of others." The word comes from the French meaning: "illusion, glamour" and in Latin it means, "tricks." Does the mind create an illusion, does it trick itself into self-belief? Why do we need a self-image? What purpose does it serve? Why do we want to be someone? We are all so self-assertive, or at least we seem so, we put on a facade of self-assurance. We feel we need to be so confident. Are we just afraid that others will take advantage of us if we aren't confident? Is the competition for work so strong that we are afraid to show a trace of weakness?

I, too, have been heavily conditioned to be confident, proud. I, too, have a strong self-image and seeing this I am aware of its power, its domination, how the image controls life, the reactions and defenses it uses to protect itself. I have seen this self-image reinforced in the Martial Arts, especially by those people who had few ways of proving themselves in society. If our practice of Karate is worth anything then it must address this issue of self-image because it is at the core of our discontent. Otherwise, taking Karate will only compound this problem, for the self-image will draw its pride from our accomplishment in our training. We must be very careful and alert to this need of the self. It is the most dangerous thing! This does not mean that we should do away with the self or feel bad about ourselves. This is just another reaction of the self and only perpetuates the destruction. It seems that the only thing we can do is to be aware of it, to observe it in action, to see and understand its structure, how it comes into being, to see the nature of it.

What happens when we observe thought (which is the self-image, the self-image having been made up through experience, through what people have told us about ourselves)? The self-image is a collection of thoughts and experiences, which combine to make up memory. This accumulation of experiences came about through time; it is the past. It is who we think we are, it is what we want life to be, it is our beliefs, ideals, our particular cultural idiosyncracies. All this is me, the "I" who tries to mold life to its desires, its expectations, and fears. Can we actually see this; not because it is written in a book, but for ourselves? Can we observe our own minds? Can we can see our own particular self-image which is the universal self-image? It is not my mind or your mind—it is mind, for the mind is common to all human beings; what makes it seem different is the particular superficial cultural influences, but what is universal is that all minds work the same, all have the ability to develop self-images. What happens now that we see this? What state of mind is there when one is seriously interested in this urgent concern? If we are observing mind, we are aware, we are intelligent and in that intelligence there is a dignity that is not of the self-image.

"The meek shall inherit the earth." We have heard this before and we either reject it or we cling to it for security, for some hope we have been given by some religion. But do we really know what it means? If we are to practice Karate intelligently is it vital that we understand what we are doing, because we could be playing with fire.

Let's look at the significance of this saying. What is the key to understanding it? Perhaps it is the word "meek" that needs to be examined. When we hear the word "meek" what comes to mind..."weak"? Does the meek sound too mild for us? Do we really feel inside that it is not the meek but the powerful that will inherit the earth, that we need to be very strong to battle the enemy? Let's look deeper at this word. Meek also means humble. The word humble has many contradictory meanings. It means, according to the American College Dictionary, "gracious, modest, mild, polite, gentle, respectful" and the like. It also means, "plain, common, ordinary, inferior, timid, despicable." It also means to "disgrace, shame, scorn, crush, destroy, defeat utterly, obliterate, smash, conquer." It is amazing how many different connotations this word has, and therefore it is understandable how we can have so many diverse opinions about this saying.

But let's look closer. Meek means, "gentle, kind, mild." Not very strong sounding. Yet it also means, "yielding." Yielding means, "to give up or surrender (oneself)." Perhaps here is the key.

Gichin Funakoshi, the father of modern Karate-do, said, "To subdue the enemy without fighting is the highest skill." To "subdue" the enemy means that we end conflict without fighting. But how? Does this saying have any relationship to "The meek shall inherit the earth"?

I think that the key is in the words "subdue" and "yield," that they are pointing to the same thing. We must be careful here and not get caught up in the words. This is not an intellectual game.

The word "yield" means to give up or surrender (oneself).

Again, this connotation may not feel right to us. We don't want to give up and surrender because we will be taken over by the "enemy." Is this what it is saying? I think not. There is a paradox here in that the words "meek," "subdue" or "yield" are not weak at all, that in fact the opposite is true.

If we are to understand the qualities of meekness, we must also understand that being subdued and yielding are actually qualities of the highest order of strength, qualities that can "defeat the enemy." Then we must look at what real strength is. Can we do this together? What shall we do to discover the qualities of strength in us? Can we learn it from another? Or are we only able to see it for ourselves? If so, where do we look?

Perhaps the place to look is our own mind. If the mind is the seat of power and strength, we need to observe what our views are about strength to see if they are actually true.

What are our images of strength? Are they the images of John Wayne, Rambo, Chuck Norris, Bruce Lee, Sumo wrestlers, boxers, war heroes? Are their images strength? We have talked about this issue time and time again. We are approaching it from a different angle this time. Can we see that these images of strength are actually weak? We believe strength to be having a self-image of confidence, of power, but when we look we see that these images are *only* images, they are *only* thoughts and not real strength. We are pretending to be strong by identifying with the popularized commercial images the media is using to exploit our need for power.

Then what is strength? These images of strength only make up our self-image, as we have talked about before. This self-image is actually a pretense of strength and therefore weak. It makes sense to be free of that which makes us weak, which is our self-image. Is there real strength when one is free of the images one has about oneself? Is this what is meant by being meek, yielding, subduing the enemy without fighting?

Does the clenched fist represent a clenched mind?

Why do we want to execute full power techniques?

Why do we talk about this style over that style? Take Nami Do is not a style that is better than another. Take Nami Do's approach is to focus on the source of conflict. Our intention is to end conflict, not to perpetuate it through our training. Anyone can do this, in any style or without ever studying the Martial Arts. Take Nami Do is only a context that creates a direct confrontation with ourselves and in so doing brings about learning.

Some people think that Karate is violent. It <u>is</u> if it emanates from hurt and the reaction of anger or from wanting to be someone which is perpetuating the self image. But in its pure form the movements of the Art of Karate are elemental, like the forces of nature and are therefore not violent.

If we think that our elemental impulses are violent we are apt to repress them. This then becomes a moral issue, a question of what is bad and good. Can we create a trusting place where we can allow these impulses to be fully explored? This doesn't mean that one has the license to vent rage on another. Expression is not a reaction nor is it a careless purging of one's inhibited emotional state.

Lightning strikes, an earthquake hits with full force, a tornado's great mass of energy explodes in a whirlwind of power. This is tremendous intensity unleashed. This is nature. Since we are a part of nature we have great energy also. Unfortunately we have been conditioned to repress this elemental energy. Perhaps if this energy were to be naturally released then we would not be violent. This elemental energy is often mistaken for violence and is therefore seen as evil, uncivilized and in need of controlling or subduing.

When we free style we hold back our energy, our passion. We hold back because we are thinking of winning or losing. Because we do this we become afraid of hurting or being hurt. When there is no thought of winning or losing or of being hurt or hurting, then there is the natural expression of passion, the elemental impulses of our nature. Since it is pure and without a motive it is not violent.

The Art of Karate brings us out, it allows us to come into direct contact with violence. There are some people who are afraid of what they think is violence and study the Martial Arts to avoid contact with this reality. They set up the ideal of nonviolence and pursue that and in so doing cause conflict and violence.

Karate, if studied seriously, develops the gentleman and the gentlewoman. Being a gentleman or gentlewoman means more than being gentle. It is a way of life that has great dignity. Dignity comes with intelligence. Intelligence is not intellect. Intelligence is sensitivity. The intellect is the ability to manipulate symbols, to analyze and synthesize information. This has its place in science and technology. What we need is intelligence that uses the intellect with care, responsibly. This is the Art of Karate, for it develops the whole person, a person who is truly educated.

Take Nami Do is not comparing itself with any style. Take Nami Do Karate is not for or against anything. We are concerned with intelligence, with living sanely in an insane world. Any serious person is interested in this whether he or she studies Take Nami Do Karate or any style of Martial Art.

Take Nami Do Karate is not a new philosophy or psychology. It has nothing to do with the "New Age." It is only a means by which one can come to understand fear, which is the compulsion underlying violence.

Philosophy means the "love of truth in everyday life." It does not mean *my* philosophy, *my* beliefs, *my* opinions, *my* way of life. This is divisive thinking and therefore creates conflict. In Take Nami Do Karate the intention is to understand why the mind, thought, creates this division as the me and mine, you and yours, we and ours, they and theirs. We are interested in finding out the truth of the matter. We are not interested in asserting our dogmatic views.

If we are to really understand self-defense in Karate, we must see what motivates the need for it.

Does the mind respond to a psychological threat as if it were a biological threat? Does it only feel threat and therefore only react in a fight or flight response? Reacting to a biological threat is necessary for survival, to keep from being physically hurt. But reacting to a psychological threat, from being hurt psychologically, is another matter. Why do we protect ourselves psychologically; who is protecting and what is it that it is protecting? If the mind cannot distinguish between the biological and psychological threat are we killing ourselves and others over our fear of being hurt psychologically? Does this fundamental issue have global implications?

Does the confidence we find in studying Karate give us the confidence to look at our need to study this Art or is the confidence only necessary for feeling secure from physical attack? How serious is our training?

Do the Martial Arts really create the condition for learning? Are we fooling ourselves into believing that we are serious? What is our real motivation behind all this? Is it just another way to enhance ourselves?

The Black Belt is a symbol of recognition, of attaining a certain proficiency in learning self-defense skills. Is it also a reflection of who we are, of our beliefs, our need for power? The Black Belt is actually only a piece of dyed cotton. Do we see all that the mind, the self, has invested in it; do we see how important it has become, how we feel when we wear it? The Black Belt, for the serious student, becomes a means for self-discovery at the deepest levels.

Karate is like the elemental forces in nature; it is like lightning, wind, thunder, a tornado, a tidal wave. It is also still like the pond, serene as floating clouds. Where in all this is the place of thought, of the self, of me?

In the complete giving up of the self, there is strength.

Can we be so sensitive as to see the potential for attack before it manifests in the mind of the other and in so doing end it before it has a chance to manifest itself? Can we also see clearly the potential for reaction in ourselves, to defend and counter-attack and in so doing end it?

One must ask the right questions and not seek answers. Asking the right questions leads to observation and insight. Seeking answers, the mind gets caught up in a maze of contradictory opinions and therefore is incapable of acting intelligently.

Making a correct technique, such as a punch, is a complex balance of bringing together many parts into a coordinated whole. Making a correct fist and wrist, properly twisting the arm as the fist moves towards the target, keeping the head steady and upright, chest out, shoulders back, having the correct stance, making correct eye contact, having a good balance and stability, bending the knees correctly, twisting the hips at the proper moment, having the proper timing and coordination, being flexible, moving from your hara (lower abdomen), having the correct balance of tension and relaxation, having the proper breath control or kiai, correct moving and changing, being ready for a counter-attack, having a clear and concentrated mind, having a resolute spirit— all this and more goes into one single punch. Yet if one doesn't understand the deeper issues, having a fundamental insight into the cause of conflict, all this excellent training will just be used to perpetuate violence, for it will turn against the student because of the student's lack of understanding; it will be used to further self-centered action and therefore continue to cause division among people.

Does your training include understanding the necessity for kara— for empty? Do we only want to develop ourselves physically, to be able to compete, to get rank? I find very few serious students in Karate who really want to understand Karate as "empty self." Most people seem to look to Karate for selfish reasons. If they only knew the tremendous joy in understanding what this "empty self" means, the significance it has in life! Training in the physical aspects of Karate has its place and is very enjoyable, but it cannot compare to the other.

If we get attached to our training, if we become so single-minded in our purpose, if we follow without question the tradition of our style, then we will destroy the essence of our practice, which is spirit, the life force. It seems that we must create a fine balance between the old and new, keeping what is necessary and being able to refine it as we go, to give new life to it. It is only our intelligence that will know what to do; this has nothing to do with our conformity to the known. We have to leave the known and step into the unknown, without the comfort of the security of what has been before.

It is not fear that is the problem. The problem is in thinking that fear is something separate from thought, that fear is real, that it has a reality independent of thought. The problem is our identification with the thought, our mistaken notion that it is reality.

We live in a dream world, of kings and queens, of princes and princesses, of warriors and villains. We are asleep, living out our collective nightmare. What will wake us up? Do we even see that we are asleep? Being in the dream world we recreate and carry on the mythical struggle of good and evil. When we train, who are we identifying with...the hero or the victim?

Are we attached to our practice, our style, our master, our sensei? If I give up these attachments, who and what will I be?

The word, "nothing" has a frightening connotation to most of us. "Death," "emptiness," "darkness," "not being" are images the mind conjures up. Can we see the mind's projections of fear? Do we identify with them and call them me? What does the mind do when someone asks, "Can you live as nothing, a nobody?"

When we take thought for reality, when we believe fear to be independent of thought, we become identified with fear, and in so doing we set into motion a self-fulfilling prophecy. "I am afraid, therefore there is something out there that is making me afraid; so the world is a fearful place, which is why I am afraid."

When thoughts of fear enter the mind can we just observe them without identification, without becoming attached to them as me? When there is no identification, these thoughts pass through the mind, but we are not affected by them. Being not affected is freedom. Freedom is nothing more than a state of non-identification with thinking.

If we talk to young people as our friends,
if we can learn together about life,
not asserting our authority, but rather offering it to them,
maybe we can bring about a wanting in them to understand themselves,
a joy, an intent in learning itself.
Perhaps the Art of Karate
can be a vehicle for this affectionate exploration.

Part V
TAKE NAMI DO
THE ART OF KARATE AND YOUNG PEOPLE

"The Art of Karate aids us in understanding violence. Too often violence has been portrayed as an heroic cultural ideal, one that upholds fighting as the honorable solution to conflict. Paradoxically one can transform hostile aggression by the means of the Art of Karate. By teaching self-defense skills to the student, one gives him or her the confidence not to fight. At the same time the student learns how to intelligently avoid conflict through using alternative, nonviolent means. In this way the young person is learning that violence is not an acceptable means of solving the problems of relationship. He or she sees that conflict is resolvable through understanding and creatively dealing with the problem."

—Terrence Webster-Doyle

Being a Martial Artist for over twenty-five years, a parent of four daughters, an Educator/Psychologist and someone who has worked in Juvenile Delinquency Prevention, I am acutely aware of the violence our children are exposed to every day. I am also aware that there is little being done to help young people cope with violence, the fight or flight situations they are confronted with at their schools, at home, and in their communities.

There is a tremendous amount of violence in our world, as anyone can see. Violence on television, in films, newspapers and magazines is all too often being portrayed as an heroic cultural ideal, one that says fighting is the honorable solution to conflict. Currently there is a new and terrifying upsurge of Martial Arts violence—a special form and breed of malicious mayhem. A great number of people, especially young people, are being trained as skillful and lethal "fighting machines." Many imitation Karate films are just beginning to hit the mass media, according to the many Martial Arts magazines. Martial Arts schools, classes and tournaments are growing rapidly. Perhaps this interest in Martial Arts, especially in Karate, is a result of the mistaken understanding that in order to combat violence and aggression, a person has to "be prepared," that is, "fight fire with fire." This is seen also in the rampant sale of guns and Martial Arts weapons. It is the "arms race" theory. But it doesn't work! It can temporarily contain violence, but it will explode sooner or later. Violence, approached in this manner, can produce only more violence.

Merely "arming" oneself doesn't solve the problem, it only dangerously compounds it. I have developed an approach for working with young people that paradoxically uses Karate to transform violence into the qualities of gentleness, kindness, and respect. Whereas the conventional approach in the Martial Arts is an "eye for an eye," with an emphasis on fighting, the Art of Karate encourages and teaches nonviolent means to solving conflict.

In the Art of Karate the intent is to help young people study self-defense skills in order to give them the confidence not to fight. In order to accomplish this we teach them how to nonviolently and creatively avoid hostile aggression through role-playing. Some examples of nonviolent solutions are: making friends, using humor, trickery, walking away, agreeing (with insult), refusing to fight, standing up (to a bully), screaming/yelling (kiai), ignoring, using authority, reasoning or talking it out, taking a (Karate) stance.

We also create a trusting environment so our students can release both normal, healthy aggression and the tension of stress within the Karate form. Techniques and exercises such as yoga, guided fantasy, sensory awareness, tension reduction, breath control and meditation are also used to aid in this process.

Lastly we help our students understand the causes of violence and aggression through the use of stories, games and activities.

I feel it is vital to include this training in the Art of Karate within the traditional school setting so young people can have the opportunity to not only learn an excellent form of individual, lifelong fitness but at the same time, have the chance to learn to resolve conflict nonviolently. If we are going to raise healthy and well-balanced children we need to educate them to understand themselves, understand relationship. Education needs to include the whole child, the emotional and physical as well as the intellectual. It needs to help children develop relationships that are sane and cooperative. As it is, relationship is primarily based on individualism, on competition and self-centered interest.

Can we raise children to be intelligent, to be skilled academically and vocationally, and at the same time be psychologically aware? Or are we mainly concerned with educating children to get ahead, to become someone, to be something? As parents and teachers we are confronted with the challenge of raising young people in a time of immense violence. Being serious, we want them to be healthy and loved. It seems perhaps an overwhelming task in the face of the global situation. But we have only our best to do. We can start where we are, with our own children. We can create educational environments that help them to be sane and intelligent human beings. We need to be in touch with other adults who are like-minded, who want to give their children a complete education so that they can survive in this world of confusion. I feel that even a small group of concerned and dedicated people, who have the intent to understand themselves and to help their children to do likewise, could change the course of human events. The Art of Karate can be one way to help make this happen.

AUTHOR'S NOTE

Finishing this book I realize the danger of writing it. The first danger is that I might be viewed as an authority. I realize that my reason for writing this book is not to be an authority but rather to put forth some observations we can all look at. It is my <u>intention</u> to inquire into these observations. Intention is the important factor. One doesn't always live completely what one sees but if there is intention then the possibility remains open.

Intention gives one the freedom to explore while not forming dogmatic conclusions, fixed ideas about reality. Intention keeps perception heightened, sharp. Conclusions dull the mind because they are static. Conclusions also create conflict, for perceptions that turn into conclusions become goals, ideals, images of how we should live. People can fight over conclusions, over their particular idiosyncratic ideals, the images each has according to their particular cultural and social conditioning. Intention cannot formulate ideals and therefore does not create conflict. Intention asks questions and awakens the mind. Conclusions formulate answers and live by them thus putting the mind to sleep.

The second danger is that I will take what is written as my ideal which I must now live up to. Since I have written this book, there can be pressure to act according to what it says. Again one is faced with the same dilemma—intention or conclusion. One must be careful to see the difference, for the weight of conditioning pulls one into the intellectual interpretation, into wanting to know, wanting therefore to be someone, to be secure. Thought is very clever and subtle, and one can fall unaware into the trap of self-centered thinking.

Now that this book is finished I invite your comments, for learning goes on and growth seems to be an endless unfoldment. I hope that this book has stimulated your thinking as it has mine in writing it. I sincerely appreciate your reading <u>One Encounter</u>. Thank you for taking your time to do so.

With respect,
Terrence Webster-Doyle

P.S. I leave you with one last observation, made many years ago, but timeless and universal in its significance.

*"The world is afterall
as the butterfly—
however it may be."*

—Soin

<u>One Encounter One Chance—Facing the Double-Edged Sword: The Essence of Take Nami Do Karate</u> is co-published by the Shuhari Institute, a part of the Atrium Society and North Atlantic Books.

The intention of the Shuhari Institute is to bring together people and resources that give an intelligent perspective to the Martial Arts and to disseminate thought provoking and insightful information about its creative aspects through literature, video tapes, classes, workshops and conferences. For more information please contact:

The Shuhari Institute
P.O. Box 938
Ojai, California 93023
Telephone: (805) 646-0488

The Shuhari Institute offers workshops in Southern California (Ventura/Santa Barbara Counties) and Northern California (Sonoma County). Mr. Webster-Doyle is available for workshops or conferences in your area upon request.

North Atlantic Books is the publishing program for the Society of Native Arts and Sciences, a non-profit educational corporation whose goals are to develop an ecological and cross-cultural perspective linking various scientific, social, and artistic fields, to nurture a holistic view of arts, sciences, humanities, and healing; and to publish and distribute literature on the relationship of mind, body, and nature.

Other books by Terrence Webster-Doyle:

Karate: The Art of Empty Self
Growing Up Sane — The Tragic Irony
Growing Up Sane — Part II: Raising Intelligent Children
Mind Like Moon — Mind Like Water: The Art of Karate for Young
People

Through training in the elemental movements of Karate
one's mind and body become reunified through this continual focusing.